Autonomous Robotics with ROS2 and Python

From Basics to Advanced Behavior Control for Intelligent Systems

Thompson Carter

Rafael Sanders

Miguel Farmer

Copyright © 2025

Contents

[12]

How to Scan a Barcode to Get a Repository

1. **Install a QR/Barcode Scanner** – Ensure you have a barcode or QR code scanner app installed on your smartphone or use a built-in scanner in **GitHub, GitLab, or Bitbucket.**

2. **Open the Scanner** – Launch the scanner app and grant necessary camera permissions.

3. **Scan the Barcode** – Align the barcode within the scanning frame. The scanner will automatically detect and process it.

4. **Follow the Link** – The scanned result will display a **URL to the repository.** Tap the link to open it in your web browser or Git client.

5. **Clone the Repository** – Use **Git clone** with the provided URL to download the repository to your local machine.

Chapter 1: Introduction to Autonomous Robotics

Welcome to the fascinating world of autonomous robotics! Whether you're a curious beginner taking your first steps or a seasoned professional aiming to deepen your understanding, this chapter will lay the foundation for your journey. We'll explore what autonomous robotics entails, trace its evolution, understand its significance in today's industries, and delve into why ROS2 and Python are your go-to tools for building intelligent systems. Let's embark on this exciting adventure together!

Overview of Autonomous Robotics

What is Autonomous Robotics?

Have you ever marveled at how self-driving cars navigate bustling city streets or how drones perform intricate aerial maneuvers without a human pilot? The magic behind these technologies lies in **autonomous robotics.**

Autonomous robotics refers to robots capable of performing tasks or operations without human intervention. These robots utilize a combination of sensors, artificial intelligence (AI), and advanced algorithms to perceive their environment, make decisions, and execute actions independently. Unlike traditional robots, which follow pre-programmed instructions, autonomous robots can adapt to changing conditions and unexpected obstacles, making them versatile and efficient in various applications.

Key Characteristics of Autonomous Robots:

1. **Perception:** Ability to sense and interpret the environment using sensors like cameras, LIDAR, and IMUs.

2. **Decision-Making:** Utilization of AI and machine learning algorithms to process data and make informed decisions.

3. **Mobility:** Capability to navigate through different terrains and environments.

4. **Adaptability:** Flexibility to adjust actions based on real-time feedback and changing conditions.

Real-World Examples:

- **Self-Driving Cars:** Navigate roads, avoid obstacles, and follow traffic rules autonomously.

- **Delivery Drones:** Transport goods from one location to another without human pilots.

- **Industrial Robots:** Perform tasks like assembly, welding, and packaging with minimal human oversight.

- **Healthcare Robots:** Assist in surgeries, patient care, and rehabilitation without constant human control.

Characteristics of Autonomous Robots

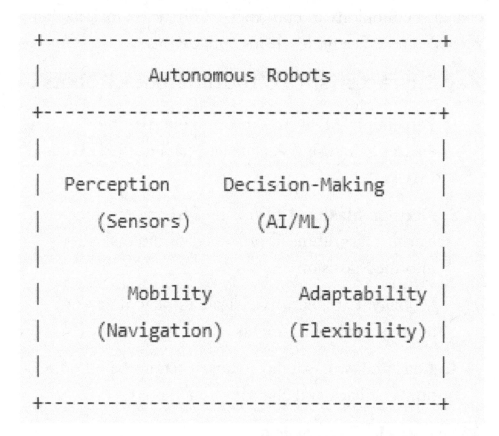

Diagram Explanation: This simple block diagram showcases the four key characteristics of autonomous robots: Perception, Decision-Making, Mobility, and Adaptability. Each characteristic is interconnected, illustrating how they work together to enable autonomy.

History and Evolution

Autonomous robotics has journeyed through decades of innovation, evolving from rudimentary machines to the sophisticated systems we see today. Understanding its history helps us appreciate the advancements and envision future possibilities.

Early Beginnings

- **1950s-1960s:** The concept of robots emerged in science fiction and early scientific research. The term "robot" was popularized by Karel Čapek's play "R.U.R." (Rossum's Universal Robots), introducing the idea of synthetic workers.

- **1961: Unimate**, the first industrial robot, was installed in a General Motors factory. This marked the beginning of robotics in manufacturing, revolutionizing assembly lines by performing repetitive and dangerous tasks with precision.

Advancements in Control Systems

- **1970s-1980s:** The development of more sophisticated control systems and the introduction of microprocessors enhanced robot capabilities. Robots became more versatile, capable of performing a wider range of tasks with improved accuracy.

- **1986: Shakey**, developed by SRI International, became the first mobile robot capable of navigating its environment and performing simple tasks autonomously. Shakey integrated perception, motion planning, and decision-making, laying the groundwork for future autonomous navigation systems.

Rise of AI and Machine Learning

- **1990s-2000s:** Integration of AI and machine learning algorithms enabled robots to process complex data, recognize patterns, and make decisions based on learned experiences. This era saw robots moving beyond pre-programmed instructions to exhibit more adaptive and intelligent behaviors.

- **2005:** The **DARPA Grand Challenge** showcased autonomous vehicles navigating challenging terrains, pushing the boundaries of autonomous navigation. Although no vehicle completed the course that year, the competition spurred significant advancements in robotics and autonomous systems.

Modern Era

- **2010s-Present:** Explosion of advancements in sensors, computing power, and AI has led to highly sophisticated autonomous robots. Self-driving cars, drones, and service robots have become more prevalent, with ongoing research focusing on enhancing autonomy, safety, and efficiency.

Timeline of Autonomous Robotics Evolution

```
+--------------------------------------------------------------+
|                 Autonomous Robotics Timeline                 |
+--------------------------------------------------------------+
| 1950s-1960s | Introduction of "robots" in literature and early |
|             | research.                                        |
|             +-----------------------------------------------+
| 1961        | Unimate, the first industrial robot, deployed.   |
|             +-----------------------------------------------+
| 1970s-1980s | Advancements in control systems and microprocessors. |
|             +-----------------------------------------------+
| 1986        | Shakey, the first mobile autonomous robot, developed. |
|             +-----------------------------------------------+
| 1990s-2000s | Integration of AI and machine learning in robotics. |
|             +-----------------------------------------------+
| 2005        | DARPA Grand Challenge accelerates autonomous vehicle |
|             | development.                                     |
|             +-----------------------------------------------+
| 2010s-Present| Proliferation of sophisticated autonomous robots, AI |
|             | advancements, and real-world applications.       |
+--------------------------------------------------------------+
```

Diagram Explanation: This timeline chart outlines the key milestones in the evolution of autonomous robotics, from the introduction of robots in the mid-20th century to the modern era of AI-driven systems.

Importance in Modern Industries

Why are autonomous robots becoming indispensable across various sectors? Let's explore their impact on key industries:

1. Manufacturing

Autonomous robots have revolutionized manufacturing by enhancing precision, efficiency, and safety.

- **Automation of Repetitive Tasks:** Robots perform tasks like assembly, welding, and painting with high accuracy, reducing human error.

- **Increased Productivity:** Continuous operation without fatigue leads to higher output and faster production cycles.

- **Safety Enhancement:** Robots handle hazardous materials and perform dangerous tasks, minimizing workplace accidents.

Example: Automotive factories utilize robotic arms for assembling vehicles, ensuring consistent quality and speeding up production lines.

2. Healthcare

In healthcare, autonomous robots assist in surgeries, patient care, and rehabilitation, improving outcomes and reducing strain on medical professionals.

- **Surgical Robots:** Perform precise surgical procedures with minimal invasiveness.

- **Rehabilitation Robots:** Aid patients in physical therapy by guiding movements and tracking progress.

- **Service Robots:** Deliver medications, manage inventories, and assist in routine tasks, allowing healthcare staff to focus on patient care.

Example: The **da Vinci Surgical System** enables surgeons to perform complex procedures with enhanced precision and control.

3. Logistics and Warehousing

Autonomous robots streamline logistics by optimizing inventory management, order fulfillment, and delivery processes.

- **Automated Guided Vehicles (AGVs):** Transport goods within warehouses, reducing the need for manual handling.

- **Inventory Management:** Robots scan and track inventory in real-time, ensuring accurate stock levels.

- **Last-Mile Delivery:** Drones and delivery robots transport packages directly to consumers, improving delivery speed and efficiency.

Example: **Amazon's Fulfillment Centers** use Kiva robots to move shelves and items, significantly reducing order processing time.

4. Agriculture

In agriculture, autonomous robots enhance farming practices by automating tasks like planting, harvesting, and monitoring crops.

- **Precision Farming:** Robots apply fertilizers and pesticides with exact precision, reducing waste and environmental impact.

- **Harvesting Robots:** Automatically pick fruits and vegetables, increasing harvesting speed and reducing labor costs.

- **Monitoring and Data Collection:** Drones and ground robots collect data on crop health, soil conditions, and weather patterns to inform farming decisions.

Example: The **Harvest CROO Robotics** strawberry picker autonomously identifies and picks ripe strawberries, boosting agricultural productivity.

5. Space Exploration

Autonomous robots play a crucial role in exploring distant planets and celestial bodies, performing tasks that are too risky or impossible for humans.

- **Rovers:** Navigate extraterrestrial terrains, collect samples, and conduct experiments.

- **Spacecraft:** Perform autonomous docking, navigation, and maintenance tasks in space.

- **Habitat Construction:** Robots assist in building structures on other planets, preparing for human habitation.

Example: **NASA's Perseverance Rover** explores Mars, searching for signs of past life and collecting geological data.

Impact of Autonomous Robotics Across Industries

```
+-----------------------------------------------------------+
|          Impact of Autonomous Robotics Across Industries  |
+-----------------------------------------------------------+
| Manufacturing   | Healthcare       | Logistics & Warehousing |
|-----------------|------------------|-------------------------|
| - Assembly lines| - Surgical robots| - AGVs in warehouses    |
| - Welding       | - Rehabilitation | - Last-mile delivery    |
| - Painting      |   robots         |   drones                |
|                 | - Service robots |                         |
+-----------------+------------------+-------------------------+
| Agriculture     | Space Exploration|                         |
|-----------------|------------------|-------------------------|
| - Precision     | - Mars rovers    |                         |
|   farming       | - Autonomous     |                         |
| - Harvesting    |   spacecraft     |                         |
|   robots        | - Habitat        |                         |
| - Monitoring    |   construction   |                         |
|   drones        |                  |                         |
+-----------------+------------------+-------------------------+
```

Diagram Explanation: This multi-section infographic illustrates the diverse applications of autonomous robotics across five major industries: Manufacturing, Healthcare, Logistics & Warehousing, Agriculture, and Space

Exploration. Each section highlights specific roles and examples of autonomous robots in action.

Why ROS2 and Python?

Choosing the right tools is crucial for developing autonomous robots. **ROS2** and **Python** have emerged as powerful allies for robotics enthusiasts and professionals alike. Let's delve into why these technologies are the preferred choices.

Introduction to ROS2

ROS2 (Robot Operating System 2) is an open-source framework that provides a collection of tools, libraries, and conventions to simplify the development of complex and robust robot behavior across a wide variety of robotic platforms.

Key Features of ROS2:

1. **Modular Architecture:** Breaks down robot functionalities into nodes, allowing for easy management and scalability.

2. **Communication Mechanisms:** Facilitates seamless communication between nodes using topics, services, and actions.

3. **Real-Time Capabilities:** Enhanced support for real-time applications, crucial for responsive robot behavior.

4. **Cross-Platform Support:** Compatible with various operating systems, including Linux, Windows, and macOS.

5. **Security Enhancements:** Built-in security features to protect data and ensure safe robot operations.

Benefits of Using ROS2:

- **Flexibility:** Easily integrate various hardware components and software modules.

- **Community Support:** A vast and active community contributes to continuous improvements and extensive documentation.

- **Reusability:** Reuse existing ROS2 packages and libraries, accelerating development.

- **Scalability:** Suitable for both small-scale projects and large, complex robotic systems.

Analogy: Think of ROS2 as the nervous system of a robot, enabling different parts to communicate and work together harmoniously.

Advantages of Using Python in Robotics

Python has become a staple in the robotics community for several compelling reasons. Let's explore why Python is the language of choice for many robotics projects.

1. Ease of Learning and Use

Python's simple and readable syntax makes it accessible to beginners and efficient for experienced programmers. This ease of use accelerates development time, allowing you to focus on solving robotics challenges rather than grappling with complex code.

2. Extensive Libraries and Frameworks

Python boasts a rich ecosystem of libraries and frameworks tailored for robotics, data processing, and machine learning.

- **NumPy & SciPy:** Essential for numerical computations and scientific computing.

- **OpenCV:** Facilitates computer vision tasks like image processing and object detection.

- **TensorFlow & PyTorch:** Powerful tools for implementing machine learning and AI algorithms.

- **Matplotlib & Seaborn:** Enable data visualization for monitoring and analysis.

3. Integration with ROS2

Python seamlessly integrates with ROS2, allowing developers to write ROS2 nodes, manage communication, and implement robot behaviors with ease. The rclpy library provides Python bindings for ROS2, making it straightforward to leverage ROS2's capabilities.

4. Rapid Prototyping

Python's flexibility and dynamic nature make it ideal for rapid prototyping. Developers can quickly test ideas, iterate on designs, and implement new features without extensive boilerplate code.

5. Strong Community and Support

A vibrant Python community ensures continuous development, abundant resources, and comprehensive support. Whether you're troubleshooting an issue or seeking best practices, the community is a valuable asset.

6. Cross-Platform Compatibility

Python runs seamlessly across various operating systems, ensuring that your robotics projects are portable and adaptable to different environments.

Real-World Example: **OpenAI's** robotics research often leverages Python for simulating environments, training AI models, and controlling physical robots, demonstrating Python's versatility and power in robotics applications.

Python and ROS2 Integration

```
+------------------------------------------------+
|                 Python and ROS2                |
+------------------------------------------------+
|                                                |
|                                                /
|   +--------------+     +--------------------+  /
|   | Python       | <-- | rclpy Library      | /
|   | Scripts      |     | (ROS2 Bindings)    | |
|   +--------------+     +---------+----------+ /
|                                  |            |
|                                  |            |
|                        +---------+------+     /
|                        | ROS2 Nodes     |     |
|                        | (Executable)   |     |
|                        +---------+------+     /
|                                  |            |
|                        +---------+------+     /
|                        | Robot Hardware|      |
|                        +---------------+      /
|                                                |
+------------------------------------------------+
```

Diagram Explanation: This flowchart illustrates how Python scripts interact with ROS2 through the rclpy library. Python scripts utilize rclpy to create ROS2 nodes, which communicate with each other and control the robot's hardware components.

Getting Started

Embarking on your journey in autonomous robotics requires setting up the right development environment and familiarizing yourself with essential tools. This section provides a clear, step-by-step guide to get you up and running.

Setting Up Your Development Environment

Creating a conducive development environment is the first step towards building autonomous robots. Here's how to set it up:

Step 1: Choose Your Operating System

While ROS2 supports multiple operating systems, **Linux (specifically Ubuntu)** is the most widely used due to its stability and compatibility with ROS2 packages.

- **Recommended OS:** Ubuntu 22.04 LTS or later

- **Alternative Options:** Windows 10/11, macOS (with limitations)

Step 2: Install Ubuntu

If you're not already using Ubuntu, consider installing it alongside your current OS or using a virtual machine.

- **Download Ubuntu:** Visit ubuntu.com to download the latest version.

- **Installation Guide:** Follow the official Ubuntu installation guide for step-by-step instructions.

Tip: Dual-booting allows you to keep your existing OS while adding Ubuntu. Alternatively, tools like VirtualBox or VMware can help you run Ubuntu in a virtual environment.

Step 3: Update Your System

Ensure your system is up-to-date to avoid compatibility issues.

```bash
```

```bash
sudo apt update
sudo apt upgrade
```

Step 4: Install Python

Ubuntu typically comes with Python pre-installed. Verify the installation:

```bash
```

```bash
python3 --version
```

If not installed, install Python 3:

```bash
```

```bash
sudo apt install python3 python3-pip
```

Note: ROS2 is compatible with Python 3, so ensure you're using the correct version.

Step 5: Install ROS2

Follow the official ROS2 installation guide tailored to your Ubuntu version. For **ROS2 Humble Hawksbill** on Ubuntu 22.04:

1. **Setup Sources:**

bash

```
sudo apt update && sudo apt install curl gnupg2
lsb-release
curl -sSL
https://raw.githubusercontent.com/ros/rosdistro/m
aster/ros.asc | sudo apt-key add -
sudo sh -c 'echo "deb
http://packages.ros.org/ros2/ubuntu $(lsb_release
-cs) main" > /etc/apt/sources.list.d/ros2-
latest.list'
```

2. **Install ROS2 Packages:**

bash

```
sudo apt update
sudo apt install ros-humble-desktop
```

3. **Source the Setup Script:**

bash

```
echo "source /opt/ros/humble/setup.bash" >>
~/.bashrc
```

```
source ~/.bashrc
```

Alternative Installation: For different ROS2 distributions or operating systems, refer to the ROS2 Installation Guide.

Step 6: Install Development Tools

You'll need essential development tools and ROS2 build tools.

```
bash
```

```
sudo apt install build-essential cmake git
sudo apt install python3-colcon-common-extensions
```

Step 7: Verify Installation

Ensure ROS2 is correctly installed by running a demo node.

1. **Run a Talker Node:**

```
bash
```

```
ros2 run demo_nodes_cpp talker
```

2. **Run a Listener Node (in another terminal):**

```
bash
```

```
ros2 run demo_nodes_cpp listener
```

You should see messages being published and received, indicating successful setup.

Troubleshooting Tip: If you encounter issues, ensure that your environment is sourced correctly (source

/opt/ros/humble/setup.bash) and that ROS2 is properly installed.

Essential Tools and Software Installation

Equipping yourself with the right tools enhances your development experience. Here are the must-have tools for autonomous robotics development with ROS2 and Python.

1. Integrated Development Environment (IDE)

An efficient IDE streamlines coding, debugging, and project management.

- **Visual Studio Code (VS Code):** Highly customizable with extensions for Python and ROS2.

Installation:

```bash
```

```
sudo snap install --classic code
```

Recommended Extensions:

- **ROS**: Provides ROS language support and commands.

- **Python**: Enhances Python development with linting, debugging, and IntelliSense.

- **C/C++**: Essential for developing ROS2 nodes in C++.

- **PyCharm:** Robust Python-specific IDE with powerful debugging and testing features.

Download from: jetbrains.com/pycharm

2. Version Control System

Managing your code versions is crucial for collaborative projects and tracking changes.

- **Git:** The most widely used version control system.

Installation:

```bash

sudo apt install git
```

Basic Git Commands:

```bash


git init          # Initialize a new Git
repository
git clone <repo>  # Clone an existing repository
git add <file>    # Add files to staging
git commit -m "Message"  # Commit changes
git push          # Push changes to remote
repository
git pull          # Pull latest changes from
remote repository
```

- **GitHub/GitLab/Bitbucket:** Platforms for hosting and collaborating on Git repositories.

Sign Up at: github.com, gitlab.com, bitbucket.org

3. ROS2 Development Tools

Enhance your ROS2 development with specialized tools.

- **RViz:** Visualization tool for ROS2, enabling real-time display of robot models, sensor data, and more.

Installation:

bash

```
sudo apt install ros-humble-rviz2
```

Usage: Launch RViz to visualize your robot's state, sensor data, and environment.

- **Gazebo:** Powerful simulation environment for testing and developing robots in virtual settings.

Installation:

bash

```
sudo apt install ros-humble-gazebo-ros-pkgs ros-humble-gazebo-ros-control
```

Usage: Simulate robot models, environments, and interactions before deploying to physical hardware.

- **Colcon:** Build tool for ROS2 packages, facilitating efficient compilation and management.

Installation:

```bash

sudo apt install python3-colcon-common-extensions
```

Basic Commands:

```bash

colcon build                  # Build all packages
in the workspace
colcon build --packages-select <package>  # Build
a specific package
colcon test                   # Run tests for all
packages
colcon test-result --verbose  # View test results
```

4. Python Libraries

Equip your Python environment with essential libraries for robotics and data processing.

- **NumPy & SciPy:** Fundamental packages for numerical computations and scientific computing.

Installation:

```bash

pip3 install numpy scipy
```

- **OpenCV:** Library for computer vision tasks, such as image processing and object detection.

Installation:

```
bash
```

```
pip3 install opencv-python
```

- **Matplotlib:** Library for creating static, animated, and interactive visualizations.

Installation:

```
bash
```

```
pip3 install matplotlib
```

- **TensorFlow & PyTorch:** Frameworks for machine learning and deep learning applications.

Installation:

```
bash
```

```
pip3 install tensorflow torch
```

Pro Tip: Use virtual environments (e.g., venv or conda) to manage your Python dependencies and avoid version conflicts.

5. Documentation and Learning Resources

Staying informed and continuously learning is vital in the ever-evolving field of robotics.

- **ROS2 Documentation:** Comprehensive guides, tutorials, and API references.

Access at: docs.ros.org/en/humble

- **Python Documentation:** Official Python documentation for in-depth language features.

Access at: python.org/doc

- **Online Courses and Tutorials:** Platforms like Coursera, Udemy, and edX offer courses on ROS2, Python, and robotics.

Essential Tools and Software Workflow

```
+--------------------------------------------------------------+
|              Development Workflow for Robotics               |
+--------------------------------------------------------------+
|                                                              |
|   +-------------+     +-------------+     +-----------+       |
|   | VS Code     | --->| Git         | --->| Colcon    |       |
|   | (IDE)       |     | (Version    |     | (Build    |       |
|   +-------------+     | Control)    |     | Tool)     |       |
|                       |             |     +-----------+       |
|                       |             |       +-----------+     |
|                       |             |       |           |     |
|                       v             v       v                 |
|            +---------------------------------------+          |
|            |              ROS2 Nodes               |          |
|            +---------------------------------------+          |
|                  |               |                            |
|                  v               v                            |
|            +----------+    +----------+                       |
|            | RViz     |    | Gazebo   |                       |
|            | (Visual  |    | (Simul   |                       |
|            | Tool)    |    | ation)   |                       |
|            +----------+    +----------+                       |
|                                                              |
+--------------------------------------------------------------+
```

Diagram Explanation: This flowchart depicts the essential development workflow for robotics projects. Code is written in an **IDE** like VS Code, managed with Git, built using Colcon, and then tested in simulation environments like Gazebo and visualized with RViz.

Overview of the Book Structure

This book is meticulously structured to guide you from the foundational concepts of autonomous robotics to advanced behavior control using ROS2 and Python. Here's what you can expect in each section:

1. **Introduction to Autonomous Robotics**

   - **What is Autonomous Robotics?**: Understand the core concepts and significance.

   - **History and Evolution:** Trace the development of robotics over the decades.

   - **Importance in Modern Industries:** Discover how various sectors leverage autonomous robots.

   - **Why ROS2 and Python?**: Learn why these tools are essential for robotics development.

   - **Getting Started:** Set up your development environment and essential tools.

2. **Fundamentals of Robotics**

   - **Basic Concepts:** Explore kinematics, dynamics, sensors, actuators, and control systems.

- ○ **Introduction to Python for Robotics**: Refresh your Python skills and learn essential libraries.

- ○ **Hands-On Project: Building Your First Simple Robot**: Apply what you've learned by assembling and programming a basic robot.

3. **Getting Started with ROS2**

  - ○ **Understanding ROS2 Architecture**: Dive into nodes, topics, services, and actions.

  - ○ **Setting Up ROS2**: Install and configure ROS2 on your system.

  - ○ **Hands-On Project: Simple ROS2 Publisher and Subscriber**: Create and test basic ROS2 communication.

4. **Sensor Integration and Data Processing**

  - ○ **Common Sensors in Robotics**: Learn about LIDAR, cameras, IMUs, and more.

  - ○ **Interfacing Sensors with ROS2**: Connect and calibrate sensors with your robot.

  - ○ **Hands-On Project: Implementing a Sensor Suite**: Equip your robot with essential sensors and visualize data.

5. **Actuator Control and Motor Management**

  - ○ **Types of Actuators**: Understand DC motors, servos, and stepper motors.

- o **Controlling Actuators with ROS2 and Python:** Implement precise motor control.

- o **Hands-On Project: Advanced Motor Control:** Integrate feedback mechanisms for enhanced control.

6. **Navigation and Mapping**

- o **Introduction to SLAM (Simultaneous Localization and Mapping):** Grasp key concepts and algorithms.

- o **Path Planning and Obstacle Avoidance:** Develop efficient navigation strategies.

- o **Hands-On Project: Building a Navigational System:** Set up SLAM and implement autonomous navigation.

7. **Behavior Control and State Machines**

- o **Understanding Behavior Trees and State Machines:** Learn about designing intelligent behaviors.

- o **Implementing Behavior Control in ROS2:** Manage state and behavior using Python.

- o **Hands-On Project: Creating Intelligent Behaviors:** Design and integrate behavior trees for task execution.

8. **Advanced Topics in Autonomous Robotics**

- o **Machine Learning and AI Integration**: Incorporate AI models into your robots.

- o **Multi-Robot Systems**: Coordinate and communicate between multiple robots.

- o **Hands-On Project: AI-Powered Object Recognition**: Train and integrate neural networks for object detection.

9. **Real-World Applications and Case Studies**

- o **Manufacturing, Healthcare, Logistics, Space Exploration**: Explore detailed case studies illustrating autonomous robotics in action.

10. **Troubleshooting and Optimization**

- o **Common Challenges**: Identify and resolve typical robotics issues.

- o **Debugging Techniques for ROS2 and Python**: Utilize tools and best practices.

- o **Optimizing Performance**: Enhance your robot's efficiency and responsiveness.

- o **Hands-On Project: Optimizing Your Robot's Performance**: Improve your robot's operations through practical solutions.

11. **Future Trends in Autonomous Robotics**

- o **Emerging Technologies**: Stay ahead with the latest advancements.

- o **The Future of ROS2**: Understand upcoming features and community growth.

- o **Preparing for the Future**: Embrace continuous learning and adapt to technological changes.

12. **Final Project: Building an Autonomous Delivery Robot**

- o **Project Overview and Objectives**: Define your project's scope.

- o **Design and Assembly**: Select components and set up hardware.

- o **Programming and Integration**: Implement navigation, behavior control, and delivery mechanisms.

- o **Testing and Deployment**: Ensure reliability and deploy your robot in real-world scenarios.

Conclusion

Embarking on the journey of autonomous robotics is both exciting and challenging. This book is designed to equip you with the knowledge, skills, and confidence to build intelligent systems capable of real-world applications. From understanding the basics to mastering advanced behavior control, each chapter provides actionable insights, hands-on projects, and real-world examples to enhance your learning experience.

Remember: Robotics is a field that thrives on curiosity, creativity, and persistence. Don't hesitate to experiment, make mistakes, and learn from them. With ROS2 and Python as your tools, you're well on your way to creating the next generation of autonomous robots.

You can do it! Let's build something amazing together.

Chapter 2: Fundamentals of Robotics

Welcome to the core of robotics! In this chapter, we'll delve into the fundamental concepts that form the backbone of any robotic system. Whether you're new to robotics or looking to solidify your understanding, this chapter will guide you through essential topics like kinematics, dynamics, sensors, actuators, and control systems. Additionally, we'll refresh your Python skills and explore the libraries that make robotics programming a breeze. By the end of this chapter, you'll not only grasp the theoretical aspects but also apply them through a hands-on project: building your very first simple robot. Let's get started!

Basic Concepts

Before we dive into the intricacies of robotics, it's crucial to understand the basic building blocks that make up a robot. Think of these concepts as the vocabulary of the robotics language. Mastering them will enable you to design, build, and program robots with confidence.

Kinematics and Dynamics

Kinematics and **dynamics** are two pillars of robotics that deal with motion. While they might sound similar, they focus on different aspects of how robots move and interact with their environment.

Kinematics

Kinematics is the study of motion without considering the forces that cause it. In robotics, kinematics involves calculating the positions, velocities, and accelerations of a robot's parts.

Key Concepts:

1. **Degrees of Freedom (DoF):**
   - Represents the number of independent movements a robot can perform.
   - Example: A robotic arm with three joints has three degrees of freedom.

2. **Forward Kinematics:**
   - Determines the position of the robot's end-effector (e.g., hand) based on joint parameters.
   - Essential for tasks like reaching a specific point in space.

3. **Inverse Kinematics:**
   - Calculates the necessary joint parameters to achieve a desired end-effector position.
   - Crucial for tasks like picking up an object from a known location.

Analogy: Imagine a person reaching out to grab a cup. Kinematics helps determine where the hand is based on the angles of the shoulder, elbow, and wrist (forward kinematics) or what angles those joints need to be at to reach the cup (inverse kinematics).

Dynamics

Dynamics goes a step further by considering the forces and torques that cause motion. In robotics, dynamics involves understanding how forces affect the robot's movement.

Key Concepts:

1. **Newton's Laws of Motion:**

   o Fundamental principles governing how forces influence motion.

   o Essential for designing robots that can interact safely and effectively with their environment.

2. **Torque:**

   o A measure of the rotational force applied to a joint.

   o Determines how much force a motor needs to move a robotic limb.

3. **Mass and Inertia:**

   o Mass affects how much force is required to accelerate or decelerate a robot's parts.

- o Inertia is the resistance of an object to changes in its state of motion.

Analogy: Think of pushing a shopping cart. Dynamics helps you understand how much force you need to apply to start moving the cart (considering its mass) or to stop it.

Kinematics vs. Dynamics

```
+----------------------------------------------+
|               Robotics Motion                |
+----------------------------------------------+

|                                              |

| Kinematics                    Dynamics       |

|  +------------------------+    +----------+ /
|  | - Degrees of        |    | - Forces| |
|  |    Freedom          |    | - Torque| |
|  | - Forward IK        |    | - Mass  | |
|  | - Inverse IK        |    | - Inertia| |
|  +------------------------+    +----------+ /

|                                              |

| Kinematics: Where and how to move?           |
| Dynamics: Why and with what force?           |

|                                              |
+----------------------------------------------+
```

Diagram Explanation: This diagram contrasts kinematics and dynamics, highlighting their core components and illustrating how they contribute to robotic motion.

Sensors and Actuators

Robots interact with the world through sensors and actuators. Sensors gather information from the environment, while actuators execute movements based on that information.

Sensors

Sensors are the eyes and ears of a robot. They allow robots to perceive their surroundings and make informed decisions.

Common Types of Sensors:

1. **Proximity Sensors:**

   - Detect the presence of nearby objects without physical contact.

   - Examples: Ultrasonic sensors, infrared sensors.

2. **Vision Sensors:**

   - Capture visual information using cameras.

   - Enable tasks like object recognition and navigation.

3. **Inertial Measurement Units (IMUs):**

   - Measure acceleration and rotation.

   - Useful for maintaining balance and orientation.

4. LIDAR (Light Detection and Ranging):

- Uses laser pulses to create detailed maps of the environment.

- Essential for autonomous navigation and obstacle avoidance.

5. Touch Sensors:

- Detect physical contact.

- Allow robots to interact safely with objects and humans.

Analogy: Imagine driving a car. Proximity sensors are like your mirrors and parking sensors, vision sensors are akin to your windshield and cameras, and IMUs are similar to your car's stability control system.

Actuators

Actuators are the muscles of a robot. They convert electrical signals into physical movement.

Common Types of Actuators:

1. Electric Motors:

- Convert electrical energy into rotational motion.

- Widely used in wheels, robotic arms, and joints.

2. Servos:

- Provide precise control over angular position.

o Ideal for applications requiring accurate movements, like steering.

3. **Stepper Motors:**

o Move in discrete steps, allowing for precise control without feedback systems.

o Commonly used in 3D printers and CNC machines.

4. **Hydraulic and Pneumatic Actuators:**

o Use fluid or air pressure to create movement.

o Suitable for heavy-duty applications requiring significant force.

Analogy: Think of actuators as the hands and legs of a robot, enabling it to grasp objects, walk, or manipulate its environment.

Sensors and Actuators Overview

```
+--------------------------------------+
|         Sensors and Actuators        |
+--------------------------------------+
|                             |
|  Sensors                    Actuators |
|  +--------------------+     +------------------+ /
|  | - Proximity    |     | - Electric    | |
|  | - Vision       |     |   Motors      | |
|  | - IMUs         |     | - Servos      | |
|  | - LIDAR        |     | - Stepper     | |
|  | - Touch        |     |   Motors      | |
|  +--------------------+     / - Hydraulic   / /
|                             |   Actuators   | |
|                             | - Pneumatic   | |
|                             |   Actuators   | |
|  +--------------------+     +------------------+ /
|  | Sensors gather |     | Actuators perform|
|  | information    |     | physical actions |
|  +--------------------+     +------------------+ /
|                             |
|  Sensors: Perceive the environment |
|  Actuators: Interact with the environment |
|                             |
+--------------------------------------+
```

Diagram Explanation: This diagram provides a side-by-side comparison of sensors and actuators, showcasing their types and roles within a robotic system.

Control Systems

Control systems are the brains that coordinate the actions of sensors and actuators, ensuring the robot behaves as intended. They process sensor data, make decisions, and send commands to actuators to achieve desired outcomes.

Types of Control Systems

1. **Open-Loop Control:**

   o Operates without feedback.

   o Commands are sent to actuators based solely on predefined instructions.

   o Simple but less accurate, as it cannot adjust to changes in the environment.

Example: A basic washing machine cycle that runs for a set time regardless of how dirty the clothes are.

2. **Closed-Loop Control (Feedback Control):**

   o Utilizes feedback from sensors to adjust actions in real-time.

   o More accurate and adaptable, as it can respond to unexpected changes.

Example: A thermostat that adjusts heating based on the current temperature.

Components of a Control System

1. **Controller:**

   o The central unit that processes input from sensors and determines the appropriate output to actuators.

- o Examples: Microcontrollers, computers running control algorithms.

2. **Sensors:**

- o Provide real-time data about the robot's state and environment.

- o Feed information into the controller for processing.

3. **Actuators:**

- o Execute the commands from the controller to perform physical actions.

- o Respond to the controller's output to achieve desired behavior.

4. **Feedback Loop:**

- o The continuous process of receiving sensor data, processing it, and adjusting actuator commands.

- o Ensures the robot maintains desired performance despite disturbances or changes.

Analogy: Imagine steering a bicycle. The controller is your brain, sensors are your eyes, and actuators are your hands turning the handlebars. If you start veering off course, your eyes detect it, your brain processes this information, and your hands adjust the handlebars to steer back.

Closed-Loop Control System

```
+-----------------------------------+
|          Controller       |
|     (Processes Input)     |
+-----------------+-----------------+
                  |
                  | Output Commands
                  v
+-----------------+-----------------+
|          Actuators        |
|     (Execute Actions)     |
+-----------------+-----------------+
                  |
                  | Physical Actions
                  v
+-----------------+-----------------+
|          Environment      |
+-----------------+-----------------+
                  ^
                  | Feedback Data
                  |
+-----------------+-----------------+
|          Sensors          |
|     (Provide Feedback)    |
+-----------------------------------+
```

Diagram Explanation: This diagram illustrates a closed-loop control system where the controller processes input from sensors, sends commands to actuators, and receives feedback from the environment to continuously adjust actions.

Introduction to Python for Robotics

Python has rapidly become a favorite programming language in the robotics community. Its simplicity, versatility, and extensive library support make it an ideal choice for both beginners and seasoned developers. In this section, we'll refresh your Python basics and explore the libraries that empower robotics programming.

Python Basics Refresher

If it's been a while since you last coded in Python, don't worry! Let's revisit some fundamental concepts to ensure you're ready to tackle robotics projects.

Variables and Data Types

Variables store information that your program can manipulate. Python supports various data types, including integers, floats, strings, and booleans.

python

```python
# Examples of variables and data types
speed = 5               # Integer
temperature = 23.5     # Float
robot_name = "RoboX"   # String
is_active = True       # Boolean
```

Control Structures

Control structures dictate the flow of your program. The most common ones are if statements and loops (for and while).

python

```python
# If statement
if speed > 10:
    print("Robot is moving fast!")
else:
    print("Robot is moving slowly.")

# For loop
for i in range(5):
    print(f"Iteration {i}")

# While loop
count = 0
while count < 5:
    print(f"Count is {count}")
    count += 1
```

Functions

Functions are reusable blocks of code that perform specific tasks. They help keep your code organized and manageable.

python

```python
def greet(name):
```

```python
    return f"Hello, {name}!"


message = greet("RoboX")
print(message)   # Output: Hello, RoboX!
```

Classes and Objects

Object-oriented programming (OOP) allows you to create objects that encapsulate data and behavior. This is particularly useful in robotics for modeling components like sensors and actuators.

```python
python


class Robot:
    def __init__(self, name):
        self.name = name
        self.speed = 0


    def move(self, speed):
        self.speed = speed
        print(f"{self.name} is moving at
{self.speed} m/s.")


    def stop(self):
        self.speed = 0
        print(f"{self.name} has stopped.")


# Creating an object
robo = Robot("RoboX")
```

```
robo.move(5)
robo.stop()
```

Python Libraries for Robotics

Python's strength lies in its rich ecosystem of libraries that extend its capabilities. Let's explore some essential libraries that are particularly useful in robotics.

NumPy & SciPy

NumPy is the foundational package for numerical computing in Python. It provides support for large, multi-dimensional arrays and matrices, along with a collection of mathematical functions to operate on these arrays.

SciPy builds on NumPy by adding a large number of higher-level functions for scientific and engineering applications.

Installation:

```bash

pip3 install numpy scipy
```

Usage Example:

```python

import numpy as np
from scipy.integrate import odeint

# Define a simple differential equation: dy/dt = -ky
```

```python
def model(y, t, k):
    dydt = -k * y
    return dydt


# Initial condition
y0 = 5


# Time points
t = np.linspace(0, 5, 100)


# Solve ODE
k = 0.3
y = odeint(model, y0, t, args=(k,))


print(y)
```

OpenCV

OpenCV (Open Source Computer Vision Library) is a powerful tool for image and video processing. It enables tasks like object detection, image filtering, and camera calibration.

Installation:

```bash
```

```
pip3 install opencv-python
```

Usage Example:

```python
```

```
import cv2

# Load an image
image = cv2.imread('robot.jpg')

# Convert to grayscale
gray = cv2.cvtColor(image, cv2.COLOR_BGR2GRAY)

# Display the image
cv2.imshow('Grayscale Image', gray)
cv2.waitKey(0)
cv2.destroyAllWindows()
```

TensorFlow & PyTorch

TensorFlow and **PyTorch** are leading frameworks for machine learning and deep learning. They are essential for developing AI-driven robotic behaviors, such as object recognition and decision-making.

Installation:

```bash
```

```
pip3 install tensorflow torch
```

Usage Example (TensorFlow):

```python
```

```
import tensorflow as tf

# Define a simple sequential model
```

```
model = tf.keras.Sequential([
    tf.keras.layers.Dense(10, activation='relu',
input_shape=(5,)),
    tf.keras.layers.Dense(1,
activation='sigmoid')
])


# Compile the model
model.compile(optimizer='adam',
loss='binary_crossentropy')


print(model.summary())
```

Matplotlib & Seaborn

Matplotlib and **Seaborn** are libraries for data visualization. They help in plotting graphs, visualizing sensor data, and monitoring robot performance.

Installation:

```
bash


pip3 install matplotlib seaborn
```

Usage Example:

```
python


import matplotlib.pyplot as plt
import seaborn as sns
import numpy as np
```

```python
# Generate sample data
time = np.linspace(0, 10, 100)
speed = np.sin(time)


# Plot using Matplotlib
plt.plot(time, speed)
plt.title('Robot Speed Over Time')
plt.xlabel('Time (s)')
plt.ylabel('Speed (m/s)')
plt.show()


# Plot using Seaborn
sns.lineplot(x=time, y=speed)
plt.title('Robot Speed Over Time')
plt.xlabel('Time (s)')
plt.ylabel('Speed (m/s)')
plt.show()
```

Python Libraries for Robotics Diagram

```
+-------------------------------------------------------+
|            Python Libraries for Robotics              |
+-------------------------------------------------------+
|                                                       |
|   +-----------+   +-----------+   +------------+      /
|   |  NumPy    |   | OpenCV    |   | TensorFlow|  |
|   | & SciPy   |   |           |   | & PyTorch |  |
|   +-----------+   +-----------+   +------------+     /
|        |               |               |          |
|        v               v               v          |
|   Numerical Computing   Computer Vision   ML/AI|
|        |               |               |          |
|        +---------------+---------------+          /
|                        |                          |
|                Data Visualization                 |
|                        |                          |
|            +---------------+                      /
|            | Matplotlib|                          |
|            | & Seaborn |                          |
|            +---------------+                      /
|                                                   |
+-------------------------------------------------------+
```

Diagram Explanation: This diagram illustrates the relationship between various Python libraries and their roles in robotics. NumPy and SciPy handle numerical computations, OpenCV manages computer vision tasks, TensorFlow and PyTorch facilitate machine learning and AI, while Matplotlib and Seaborn are used for data visualization.

Hands-On Project: Building Your First Simple Robot

Nothing beats learning by doing. In this hands-on project, we'll guide you through building a simple robot from scratch. You'll assemble the hardware components, program basic movements using Python, and see your robot come to life!

Components Needed

Before we start assembling, let's gather all the necessary components. Don't worry if you don't have everything on hand yet; you can source these items from online retailers or local electronics stores.

Hardware Components:

1. **Microcontroller:**

    o **Raspberry Pi 4 Model B** (4GB RAM recommended)

        ▪ *Function:* Acts as the brain of the robot, running your Python scripts and managing sensors and actuators.

2. **Motor Controller:**

    o **L298N Dual H-Bridge Motor Driver Module**

        ▪ *Function:* Controls the speed and direction of the motors based on signals from the Raspberry Pi.

3. **Motors:**

   o **2 DC Motors with Wheels**

      ▪ *Function:* Provide movement for the robot. Ensure they are compatible with the motor controller.

4. **Chassis:**

   o **Basic Robot Chassis Kit**

      ▪ *Function:* Provides the structure to mount all components securely.

5. **Power Supply:**

   o **Lithium-Polymer (LiPo) Battery Pack (7.4V)**

      ▪ *Function:* Powers the motors and the Raspberry Pi.

6. **Sensors:**

   o **Ultrasonic Distance Sensor (HC-SR04)**

      ▪ *Function:* Detects obstacles in front of the robot to prevent collisions.

7. **Wiring and Connectors:**

   o **Jumper Wires and Breadboard**

      ▪ *Function:* Connect components without soldering.

8. **Miscellaneous:**

- o **Screws, Nuts, and Mounting Hardware**

- o **USB Cable for Raspberry Pi**

- o **SD Card (16GB or higher) for Raspberry Pi OS**

Software Components:

1. **Raspberry Pi OS:**

   - o *Function:* Operating system for the Raspberry Pi.

2. **Python 3:**

   - o *Function:* Programming language used to control the robot.

3. **Libraries:**

   - o gpiozero for controlling GPIO pins.

   - o time for managing delays.

Components Layout Diagram

```
+-------------------------------------------------+
|                 Robot Chassis                   |
+-------------------------------------------------+
|                                               |
|   +-------------------+   +-----------------+  /
|   | Raspberry Pi|     |   | Motor          |  |
|   |  4 Model B  |---/ | Controller/        /
|   +-------------------+   +-----------------+  /
|           |                       |           |
|           |                       |           |
|   +-------+------+       +-----+------+       /
|   | Ultrasonic   |       | DC Motors  |       |
|   | Distance     |       | with Wheels|       |
|   | Sensor       |       +------------+       /
|   +-----------+--+                            /
|               | |                           |
|       +-------+-+--------+                   /
|       |      Power       |                   |
|       |      Supply      |                   |
|       +------------------+                   /
|                                     |
+-------------------------------------------------+
```

Diagram Explanation: This layout diagram shows how the main components are arranged on the robot chassis. The Raspberry Pi connects to the motor controller, which in turn controls the DC motors. The ultrasonic sensor is positioned at the front to detect obstacles, and the power supply feeds both the Raspberry Pi and the motor controller.

Step-by-Step Assembly

Now that you have all the components, let's assemble your robot. Follow these steps carefully to ensure everything is connected correctly.

Step 1: Mounting the Raspberry Pi

1. **Secure the Raspberry Pi to the Chassis:**

   - Use the provided screws and mounting hardware to attach the Raspberry Pi to the designated area on the chassis.

   - Ensure that the GPIO pins are accessible for wiring.

2. **Install the SD Card:**

   - Insert the SD card with Raspberry Pi OS into the Raspberry Pi.

   - If you haven't installed the OS yet, download it from the official website and use a tool like Balena Etcher to flash it onto the SD card.

Step 2: Connecting the Motor Controller

1. **Attach the Motor Controller to the Chassis:**

   - Place the L298N motor driver module onto the chassis.

- o Secure it using screws or adhesive tape to prevent movement.

2. **Wire the DC Motors to the Motor Controller:**

- o Connect the two DC motors to the output terminals on the motor controller.

- o Ensure the polarity is correct to allow the motors to spin in the desired direction.

3. **Connect the Motor Controller to the Raspberry Pi:**

- o Use jumper wires to connect the input pins (IN1, IN2, IN3, IN4) on the motor controller to the GPIO pins on the Raspberry Pi.

- o Refer to the motor controller's pinout diagram to ensure accurate connections.

Step 3: Setting Up the Ultrasonic Sensor

1. **Mount the Ultrasonic Sensor:**

- o Attach the HC-SR04 ultrasonic sensor to the front of the chassis using screws or mounting tape.

- o Position it at a height that allows it to effectively detect obstacles.

2. **Connect the Ultrasonic Sensor to the Raspberry Pi:**

- o Use jumper wires to connect the sensor's VCC, GND, TRIG, and ECHO pins to the Raspberry Pi's GPIO pins.

- Example Connections:
  - VCC → 5V
  - GND → Ground
  - TRIG → GPIO23
  - ECHO → GPIO24

Ultrasonic Sensor Connection Diagram

```
+-----------------------+      +-----------------------+

| Ultrasonic Sensor |        |   Raspberry Pi GPIO |

+-----------------------+      +-----------------------+

| VCC  --------> 5V |         | Pin 2 (5V)          |
| GND  --------> GND |        | Pin 6 (GND)         |
| TRIG --------> GPIO23|        | Pin 16 (GPIO23)     |
| ECHO --------> GPIO24|        | Pin 18 (GPIO24)     |

+-----------------------+      +-----------------------+
```

Diagram Explanation: This diagram shows the connections between the ultrasonic sensor and the Raspberry Pi's GPIO pins, ensuring proper power and signal transmission.

Step 4: Connecting the Power Supply

1. **Attach the LiPo Battery to the Chassis:**

   o Secure the battery pack in a designated area on the chassis using straps or mounting brackets.

   o Ensure it's firmly in place to prevent movement during operation.

2. **Connect the Battery to the Motor Controller:**

   o Use the appropriate cables to connect the battery's positive and negative terminals to the motor controller's power input.

   o Double-check the polarity to avoid damaging the components.

3. **Powering the Raspberry Pi:**

   o Use a USB cable to connect the Raspberry Pi's power port to the motor controller's 5V output (if supported) or use a separate power source.

   o Ensure the Raspberry Pi receives a stable 5V supply to function correctly.

Safety Tip: Always disconnect the power supply before making or modifying connections to prevent short circuits or damage to components.

Step 5: Finalizing the Assembly

1. Organize the Wiring:

- o Use cable ties or adhesive tape to bundle and secure loose wires.

- o Ensure that wires do not obstruct moving parts or get tangled during robot operation.

2. Double-Check All Connections:

- o Verify that all components are connected correctly and securely.

- o Refer to the wiring diagrams provided in the previous sections to ensure accuracy.

3. Test the Physical Assembly:

- o Gently move the robot to ensure that the wheels rotate freely and that the chassis is stable.

- o Make any necessary adjustments before proceeding to programming.

Fully Assembled Robot Diagram

```
+- - - - - - - - - - - - - - - - - - - - - - - - - - - - - -+
|                    Assembled Robot                        |
+- - - - - - - - - - - - - - - - - - - - - - - - - - - - - -+
|                                                         |
|    +- - - - - - - - +      +- - - - - - - - +             /
|    | Raspberry |      | Motor      |             |
|    | Pi 4        |- - - - -| Controller|- - - - - - - - - - - - - - -|
|    +- - - - - - - - +      +- - - - - - - - +             /
|         |                    |                  |
|         |                    |                  |
|    +- - - - -+- - - - -+      +- - - - - +- - - - - +             /
|    | Ultrasonic |      | DC Motors |                  |
|    | Sensor     |      | with Wheels|                  |
|    +- - - - - - - - +-+      +- - - - - - - - +             /
|              | |                            |
|         +- - - - -+-+- - - - -+                           /
|         |    Power     |                  |
|         |    Supply    |                  |
|         +- - - - - - - - +                           /
|                                                         |
+- - - - - - - - - - - - - - - - - - - - - - - - - - - - - -+
```

Diagram Explanation: This diagram provides an overview of the fully assembled robot, showing how each component is interconnected on the chassis.

Programming Basic Movements

With the hardware assembled, it's time to bring your robot to life through programming. We'll write a simple Python script that allows your robot to move forward, backward, turn left, and turn right.

Step 1: Setting Up the Python Environment

1. **Boot Up the Raspberry Pi:**

   - Insert the SD card into the Raspberry Pi and power it on.

   - Complete the initial setup if you haven't done so already.

2. **Update and Upgrade Packages:**

Open the terminal and run:

bash

```bash
sudo apt update
sudo apt upgrade
```

3. **Install Necessary Python Libraries:**

Ensure that gpiozero is installed for controlling GPIO pins.

bash

```bash
sudo apt install python3-gpiozero
```

Step 2: Writing the Movement Script

1. **Create a New Python File:**

Open your preferred IDE (e.g., VS Code) and create a new file named robot_movement.py.

2. Import Required Libraries:

python

```python
from gpiozero import Motor
from time import sleep
```

3. Initialize the Motors:

Identify the GPIO pins connected to the motor controller's input pins.

python

```python
# Define motor pins
motor_left = Motor(forward=23, backward=24)    #
Adjust pins as per your connections
motor_right = Motor(forward=27, backward=22)   #
Adjust pins as per your connections
```

4. Define Movement Functions:

python

```python
def move_forward(duration):
    motor_left.forward()
    motor_right.forward()
    sleep(duration)
    stop()

def move_backward(duration):
    motor_left.backward()
    motor_right.backward()
```

```python
    sleep(duration)
    stop()


def turn_left(duration):
    motor_left.backward()
    motor_right.forward()
    sleep(duration)
    stop()


def turn_right(duration):
    motor_left.forward()
    motor_right.backward()
    sleep(duration)
    stop()


def stop():
    motor_left.stop()
    motor_right.stop()
```

5. Create a Simple Control Loop:

python

```python
if __name__ == "__main__":
    try:
        while True:
            command = input("Enter command (f:
forward, b: backward, l: left, r: right, s: stop,
q: quit): ").lower()
            if command == 'f':
```

```
        move_forward(2)
    elif command == 'b':
        move_backward(2)
    elif command == 'l':
        turn_left(1)
    elif command == 'r':
        turn_right(1)
    elif command == 's':
        stop()
    elif command == 'q':
        stop()
        break
    else:
        print("Invalid command.")
except KeyboardInterrupt:
    stop()
    print("\nRobot stopped.")
```

Explanation:

- **Motor Initialization:**

  - Motor(forward=23, backward=24) initializes a motor where GPIO23 controls forward motion and GPIO24 controls backward motion.

  - Adjust the **GPIO** pin numbers based on your actual connections.

- **Movement Functions:**

- o Each function commands the motors to move in a specific direction for a set duration, then stops.

- **Control Loop:**

  - o Continuously prompts the user for movement commands.

  - o Allows manual control of the robot via keyboard inputs.

Step 3: Running the Script

1. **Ensure All Connections are Secure:**

   - o Double-check that the motor controller is connected correctly to the Raspberry Pi and motors.

2. **Execute the Script:**

In the terminal, navigate to the directory containing robot_movement.py and run:

```bash
bash
```

```
python3 robot_movement.py
```

3. **Control Your Robot:**

   - o **Commands:**

     - • f – Move forward

     - • b – Move backward

- l – Turn left

- r – Turn right

- s – Stop

- q – Quit the program

  o **Example Interaction:**

```
less
```

```
Enter command (f: forward, b: backward, l: left,
r: right, s: stop, q: quit): f
Robot moves forward for 2 seconds.
Enter command (f: forward, b: backward, l: left,
r: right, s: stop, q: quit): l
Robot turns left for 1 second.
Enter command (f: forward, b: backward, l: left,
r: right, s: stop, q: quit): q
Robot stopped.
```

Troubleshooting Tips:

- **No Movement:**

  o Verify GPIO pin connections.

  o Ensure the motors are powered correctly.

  o Check that the motor controller is receiving signals from the Raspberry Pi.

- **Erratic Movement:**

  o Ensure the wiring is secure and free from shorts.

    o Verify that the power supply provides sufficient current for the motors.

Robot Movement Control Flowchart

```
+-----------------------------------------+
|              User   Input               |
+-----------------------------------------+
                    |
                    v
+-----------------------------------------+
|     Read  Command  (f,  b,  l,  r)      |
+-----------------------------------------+
                    |
                    v
+-----------------------------------------+
|    Execute  Movement  Function          |
|    (move_forward,  move_back,           |
|     turn_left,  turn_right)             |
+-----------------------------------------+
                    |
                    v
+-----------------------------------------+
|              Motors                     |
|    -  Rotate  Forward/Backward          |
|    -  Control  Speed  and  Direction    |
+-----------------------------------------+
                    |
                    v
+-----------------------------------------+
|             Robot  Moves                |
+-----------------------------------------+
                    |
                    v
+-----------------------------------------+
|              Stop                       |
+-----------------------------------------+
```

Diagram Explanation: This flowchart outlines the process from user input to the robot's movement, demonstrating how commands are read, interpreted, and executed through motor control.

Conclusion

Congratulations! You've just built your first simple robot and programmed it to perform basic movements. This hands-on experience is a significant step in your robotics journey, allowing you to apply theoretical concepts to a tangible project. As you progress, you'll explore more complex systems, integrate advanced sensors, and develop sophisticated control algorithms. Remember, the foundation you've built here is crucial for tackling more ambitious projects.

Next Steps:

1. **Experiment with Movements:**

   - Modify the durations in the movement functions to see how your robot's speed and turning angles change.

   - Implement new movement patterns, such as zig-zagging or circular paths.

2. **Integrate Additional Sensors:**

   - Add more sensors like infrared or camera modules to enhance your robot's perception.

   - Use sensor data to create autonomous behaviors, such as obstacle avoidance.

3. **Explore Advanced Python Libraries:**

- o Dive deeper into libraries like OpenCV for computer vision or TensorFlow for machine learning.

- o Implement features like object recognition or path planning.

4. **Expand Your Control System:**

- o Transition from manual control to autonomous control using feedback from sensors.

- o Implement PID (Proportional-Integral-Derivative) controllers for smoother and more precise movements.

Remember: Robotics is a field that thrives on experimentation and continuous learning. Don't hesitate to try new ideas, face challenges head-on, and seek out resources to expand your knowledge. With each project, you'll gain valuable insights and skills that will empower you to build more intelligent and capable robots.

You're well on your way to becoming a robotics pro! Keep pushing the boundaries, and enjoy the journey of creating machines that can perceive, think, and act autonomously.

Summary

In Chapter 2, "Fundamentals of Robotics," we explored essential concepts that form the foundation of any robotic system. We delved into kinematics and dynamics, understanding how robots move and interact with their environment. We examined the critical roles of sensors and actuators in enabling robots to perceive and act, and we unpacked the intricacies of control systems that coordinate these components.

Additionally, we refreshed our Python programming skills and explored key libraries like NumPy, SciPy, OpenCV, TensorFlow, and Matplotlib, which are indispensable tools for robotics development. Finally, through a hands-on project, we built and programmed a simple robot, applying the theoretical knowledge to create a functioning machine capable of basic movements.

This chapter not only provided you with the theoretical underpinnings of robotics but also empowered you with practical skills to start building your own robots. As you move forward, these fundamentals will serve as the building blocks for more advanced topics and complex projects in the exciting field of autonomous robotics.

Chapter 3: Getting Started with ROS2

Welcome to the next step in your robotics journey! Now that you've grasped the fundamentals of robotics and built your first simple robot, it's time to dive into **ROS2 (Robot Operating System 2)**. ROS2 is a powerful framework that simplifies the development of complex robotic systems, enabling seamless communication between different components. Whether you're aiming to build sophisticated autonomous robots or enhance existing systems, ROS2 is your gateway to achieving these goals. Let's explore ROS2's architecture, understand its core components, set up your development environment, and embark on a hands-on project to create your first ROS2 nodes.

Understanding ROS2 Architecture

Imagine ROS2 as the central nervous system of a robot, orchestrating the interactions between various components to ensure smooth and coordinated behavior. To appreciate ROS2's power, it's essential to understand its architecture and the key concepts that underpin it.

Nodes, Topics, Services, and Actions

At the heart of ROS2 lie four fundamental concepts: **nodes, topics, services,** and **actions.** These elements work together to facilitate communication and coordination within robotic systems.

Nodes

Nodes are the fundamental building blocks of ROS2. Each node represents a single process that performs a specific function within the robot. Think of nodes as individual departments within a company, each handling a particular task.

- **Example:** In a robot, you might have separate nodes for controlling the wheels, processing camera images, and managing sensor data.

Key Points:

- **Modularity:** Nodes allow you to break down complex systems into manageable, independent units.

- **Scalability:** You can add or remove nodes without affecting the entire system.

- **Flexibility:** Nodes can be written in various programming languages, though Python and C++ are the most common.

Topics

Topics are the channels through which nodes communicate asynchronously. They enable nodes to publish and subscribe to streams of data, fostering a decoupled and flexible communication pattern.

- **Publisher:** A node that sends messages to a topic.

- **Subscriber:** A node that listens for messages on a topic.

Example: A camera node publishes images to a /camera/image topic, while a processing node subscribes to this topic to analyze the images.

Key Points:

- **Many-to-Many Communication:** Multiple publishers and subscribers can interact on the same topic.

- **Asynchronous Communication:** Publishers and subscribers operate independently, without waiting for responses.

- **Data Streams:** Topics handle continuous streams of data, making them ideal for real-time applications.

Services

Services facilitate synchronous, request-response communication between nodes. They are useful for operations that require a definite reply or confirmation.

- **Service Server:** A node that offers a service.

- **Service Client:** A node that requests a service.

Example: A navigation node might offer a /navigate service, allowing other nodes to request the robot to move to a specific location.

Key Points:

- **Synchronous Communication:** The client waits for a response from the server.

- **One-to-One Interaction:** Each service request is handled by a single server.

- **Defined Contracts:** Services have well-defined request and response message structures.

Actions

Actions extend the service concept by supporting long-running tasks with feedback and the ability to cancel operations. They are ideal for tasks that take an extended period to complete.

- **Action Server:** A node that performs the action.

- **Action Client:** A node that requests the action.

Example: An arm movement node might offer an /arm_move action, allowing other nodes to command the robot's arm to move while receiving real-time feedback on its progress.

Key Points:

- **Asynchronous Communication:** Clients can send goals and continue operating while the server processes them.

- **Feedback and Result:** Clients receive ongoing feedback and a final result upon completion.

- **Cancelable Goals:** Clients can cancel actions if needed.

ROS2 Communication Concepts Diagram

```
+------------------+        +------------------+         +------------------+
|    Node A        |        |     Topics       |         |    Node B        |
|  (Publisher)     |---------->|  /sensor/data  |<----------|  (Subscriber)   |
+------------------+        +------------------+         +------------------+


+------------------+        +------------------+         +------------------+
|    Node C        |        |    Services      |         |    Node D        |
| (Service Client) |---------->|  /get_status   |<----------| (Service Server)|
+------------------+        +------------------+         +------------------+


+------------------+        +------------------+         +------------------+
|    Node E        |        |    Actions       |         |    Node F        |
| (Action Client)  |---------->|  /arm_move     |<----------| (Action Server) |
+------------------+        +------------------+         +------------------+
```

Diagram Explanation: This diagram illustrates the interaction between different nodes using topics, services, and actions. Node A publishes data to /sensor/data, which Node B subscribes to. Node C requests a service from /get_status, which Node D provides. Node E initiates an action /arm_move, handled by Node F.

ROS2 Communication Mechanisms

Effective communication is pivotal in robotics, ensuring that different components work in harmony. ROS2 offers robust communication mechanisms that cater to various interaction patterns, enhancing flexibility and scalability.

Data Serialization

Before transmitting data, ROS2 serializes messages into a format suitable for transmission over networks. Serialization converts complex data structures into a byte stream, ensuring consistency and compatibility across different systems.

- **Protocol Buffers (Protobuf):** ROS2 uses Protobuf for message serialization, providing efficient and language-agnostic data representation.

Key Points:

- **Efficiency:** Serialized data reduces transmission overhead.

- **Interoperability:** Ensures that different nodes, possibly written in different languages, can understand the data.

- **Extensibility:** Easily accommodates changes and additions to message structures.

Middleware Abstraction

ROS2 abstracts the underlying middleware, allowing developers to choose the most suitable communication layer based on their application's needs. This abstraction enhances flexibility and performance.

- **DDS (Data Distribution Service):** The default middleware for ROS2, DDS offers high performance, scalability, and real-time capabilities.

Benefits of DDS:

- ○ **QoS (Quality of Service) Policies:** Control aspects like reliability, durability, and latency.

- ○ **Scalability:** Supports large-scale systems with numerous nodes.

- ○ **Real-Time Performance:** Suitable for time-sensitive applications.

Key Points:

- **Flexibility:** Developers can switch middleware implementations without altering ROS2-based code.

- **Customization:** DDS allows fine-tuning communication parameters to meet specific requirements.

- **Interoperability:** Facilitates seamless integration with other DDS-based systems.

ROS2 Middleware Interface (RMW)

ROS2's middleware interface (RMW) allows seamless integration with different DDS implementations. This interface ensures that ROS2 can leverage the strengths of various middleware solutions without compromising on functionality.

- **Popular DDS Implementations:**

  - ○ **Fast DDS:** Known for its high performance and low latency.

  - ○ **Cyclone DDS:** Emphasizes reliability and real-time performance.

  - ○ **Connext DDS:** Offers advanced features and extensive support.

Key Points:

- **Pluggable Architecture:** Easily swap out DDS implementations based on project needs.

- **Performance Optimization:** Choose middleware that best suits the performance and reliability requirements.

- **Community and Support:** Leverage the strengths and support of various DDS communities.

ROS2 Communication Flow Diagra

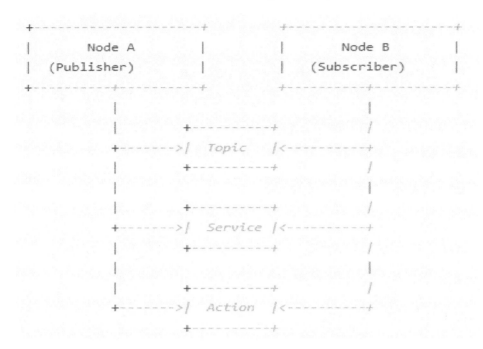

Diagram Explanation: This diagram showcases how nodes communicate using topics, services, and actions. Node A can publish data to a topic that Node B subscribes to, request a service from Node C, or initiate an action with Node D.

Setting Up ROS2

Now that you understand the architecture and communication mechanisms of ROS2, it's time to set up your development environment. This section will guide you through installing ROS2 on different operating systems and creating your first ROS2 package.

Installation Guide for Different Operating Systems

ROS2 supports multiple operating systems, but the most seamless experience is on Linux, specifically Ubuntu. Below, we'll cover installation steps for Ubuntu, Windows, and macOS.

Installing ROS2 on Ubuntu

Ubuntu is the recommended operating system for ROS2 due to its compatibility and support. Follow these steps to install ROS2 on Ubuntu 22.04 LTS (Jammy Jellyfish).

Step 1: Setup Sources

1. **Update Your System:**

Open the terminal and run:

bash

```
sudo apt update && sudo apt upgrade
```

2. **Add the ROS2 Repository:**

Import the ROS2 GPG key:

bash

```
sudo apt install software-properties-common
sudo add-apt-repository universe
sudo apt update && sudo apt install curl gnupg2
lsb-release
```

```
curl -sSL
https://raw.githubusercontent.com/ros/rosdistro/m
aster/ros.asc | sudo apt-key add -
sudo sh -c 'echo "deb
http://packages.ros.org/ros2/ubuntu $(lsb_release
-cs) main" > /etc/apt/sources.list.d/ros2-
latest.list'
```

Step 2: Install ROS2 Packages

1. Update the Package Index:

```
bash
```

```
sudo apt update
```

2. Install ROS2 Humble Hawksbill:

```
bash
```

```
sudo apt install ros-humble-desktop
```

Note: The desktop installation includes essential tools like RViz, Gazebo, and demos.

Step 3: Environment Setup

1. Source the Setup Script:

Add the ROS2 setup script to your shell startup file:

```
bash
```

```
echo "source /opt/ros/humble/setup.bash" >>
~/.bashrc
source ~/.bashrc
```

2. Install Additional Dependencies:

bash

```
sudo apt install python3-argcomplete
```

Step 4: Verify the Installation

Run a demo to ensure ROS2 is correctly installed.

1. Launch ROS2 Talker Node:

bash

```
ros2 run demo_nodes_cpp talker
```

2. Launch ROS2 Listener Node (in another terminal):

bash

```
ros2 run demo_nodes_cpp listener
```

Expected Output: The listener node should receive and display messages from the talker node, indicating successful communication.

Installing ROS2 on Windows

Installing ROS2 on Windows allows for development in a Windows environment, though it may require additional configuration.

Prerequisites:

- **Windows 10 (64-bit) or later**

- Visual Studio 2019 or later (with Desktop development with C++ workload)

- Python 3.8 or later

Step 1: Install Chocolatey Package Manager

1. Open PowerShell as Administrator:

2. Run the Following Command:

```
powershell


Set-ExecutionPolicy Bypass -Scope Process -Force;
`
[System.Net.ServicePointManager]::SecurityProtoco
l = `
[System.Net.ServicePointManager]::SecurityProtoco
l -bor 3072; `
iex ((New-Object
System.Net.WebClient).DownloadString('https://cho
colatey.org/install.ps1'))
```

Step 2: Install ROS2 Humble

1. Install Dependencies:

```
powershell


choco install -y git cmake wget
```

2. Download the ROS2 Installer:

Visit the ROS2 Downloads page and download the appropriate installer.

3. Run the Installer:

Follow the on-screen instructions to complete the installation.

Step 3: Environment Setup

1. **Open a New Command Prompt as Administrator.**

2. **Source the ROS2 Environment:**

cmd

```
call C:\dev\ros2_humble\local_setup.bat
```

Step 4: Verify the Installation

Run a demo to ensure ROS2 is correctly installed.

1. **Launch ROS2 Talker Node:**

cmd

```
ros2 run demo_nodes_cpp talker
```

2. **Launch ROS2 Listener Node (in another Command Prompt):**

cmd

```
ros2 run demo_nodes_cpp listener
```

Expected Output: The listener node should receive and display messages from the talker node.

Installing ROS2 on macOS

ROS2 on macOS is less straightforward compared to Ubuntu and Windows but is still achievable with careful configuration.

Prerequisites:

- macOS Catalina (10.15) or later
- Homebrew Package Manager
- Xcode Command Line Tools

Step 1: Install Homebrew

1. Open Terminal and Run:

bash

```
/bin/bash -c "$(curl -fsSL
https://raw.githubusercontent.com/Homebrew/instal
l/HEAD/install.sh)"
```

Step 2: Install Dependencies

1. Install Dependencies:

bash

```
brew install cmake python3 wget
```

Step 3: Install ROS2 Humble

1. Download ROS2 Humble:

Visit the ROS2 Downloads page and download the appropriate package.

2. Extract and Install:

Follow the instructions provided on the ROS2 installation page for macOS.

Step 4: Environment Setup

1. Source the ROS2 Setup Script:

Add the ROS2 setup script to your shell startup file (e.g., .bash_profile or .zshrc):

bash

```
echo "source /opt/ros/humble/setup.bash" >>
~/.zshrc
source ~/.zshrc
```

Step 5: Verify the Installation

Run a demo to ensure ROS2 is correctly installed.

1. Launch ROS2 Talker Node:

bash

```
ros2 run demo_nodes_cpp talker
```

2. Launch ROS2 Listener Node (in another Terminal):

bash

```
ros2 run demo_nodes_cpp listener
```

Expected Output: The listener node should receive and display messages from the talker node.

ROS2 Supported Operating Systems Diagram

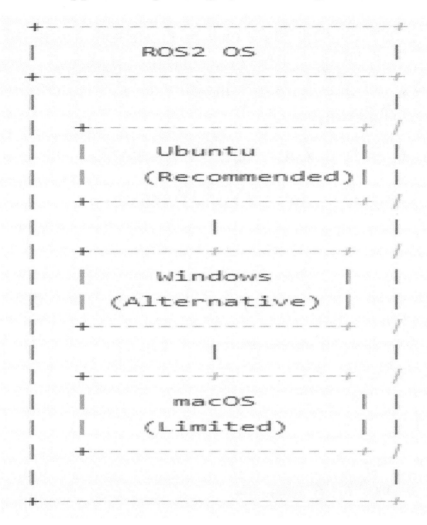

Diagram Explanation: This diagram highlights the operating systems supported by ROS2, emphasizing Ubuntu as the recommended platform while also acknowledging Windows and macOS as alternative options with varying levels of support.

Creating Your First ROS2 Package

With ROS2 installed, you're ready to create your first ROS2 package. A package in ROS2 is a collection of nodes, libraries, and other resources that work together to perform a specific function.

Step 1: Setup Your ROS2 Workspace

1. **Create a Directory for Your Workspace:**

bash

```
mkdir -p ~/ros2_ws/src
cd ~/ros2_ws/src
```

2. **Initialize the Workspace:**

bash

```
cd ~/ros2_ws/
colcon build
```

3. **Source the Workspace:**

bash

```
source install/setup.bash
```

Step 2: Create a New ROS2 Package

1. **Navigate to the Source Directory:**

bash

```
cd ~/ros2_ws/src
```

2. **Use ros2 pkg create to Generate the Package:**

bash

```
ros2 pkg create --build-type ament_python
my_robot_pkg --dependencies rclpy std_msgs
```

Explanation:

- o --build-type ament_python: Specifies that the package uses Python and the ament build system.

- o my_robot_pkg: The name of your package.

- o --dependencies rclpy std_msgs: Lists the package dependencies.

Step 3: Understand the Package Structure

Navigate into your newly created package directory:

bash

```
cd my_robot_pkg
```

Directory Structure:

```
arduino

my_robot_pkg/
├── my_robot_pkg/
│   ├── __init__.py
│   └── my_robot_pkg.py
├── resource/
│   └── my_robot_pkg
├── setup.cfg
├── setup.py
├── package.xml
└── test/
    └── test_my_robot_pkg.py
```

Key Files and Directories:

- **my_robot_pkg/:** Contains the Python modules for your package.

    - **__init__.py:** Makes Python treat the directory as a package.

    - **my_robot_pkg.py:** Your main Python script.

- **resource/:** Contains additional resources for the package.

- **setup.cfg & setup.py:** Configuration files for building and installing the package.

- **package.xml:** Defines the package metadata and dependencies.

- **test/:** Contains test scripts for your package.

ROS2 Package Structure Diagram

```
+-------------------------------------+
|            my_robot_pkg             |
+-------------------------------------+
|                                     |
|   +-----------------------------+   /
|   |  my_robot_pkg/           |   |
|   |    |-- __init__.py       |   |
|   |    '-- my_robot_pkg.py|   |
|   +-----------------------------+   /
|                                     |
|   +-----------------------------+   /
|   |  resource/               |   |
|   |    '-- my_robot_pkg     |   |
|   +-----------------------------+   /
|                                     |
|   +-----------------------------+   /
|   |  setup.cfg               |   |
|   +-----------------------------+   /
|   |  setup.py                |   |
|   +-----------------------------+   /
|   |  package.xml             |   |
|   +-----------------------------+   /
|                                     |
|   +-----------------------------+   /
|   |  test/                   |   |
|   |    '-- test_my_robot_pkg.py|
|   +-----------------------------+   /
|                                     |
+-------------------------------------+
```

Diagram Explanation: This diagram outlines the typical structure of a ROS2 Python package, highlighting the main directories and files essential for development and deployment.

Step 4: Build the Package

1. **Navigate to the Workspace Root:**

bash

```
cd ~/ros2_ws/
```

2. **Build the Workspace Using Colcon:**

bash

```
colcon build
```

Note: Colcon will compile your package and its dependencies, ensuring everything is set up correctly.

3. **Source the Setup Script:**

bash

```
source install/setup.bash
```

Step 5: Verify the Package Installation

Ensure that ROS2 recognizes your new package by listing all available packages:

bash

```
ros2 pkg list | grep my_robot_pkg
Expected Output: my_robot_pkg
```

Hands-On Project: Simple ROS2 Publisher and Subscriber

Now that you've set up ROS2 and created your first package, it's time to put your knowledge into practice. In this hands-on project, you'll create two simple ROS2 nodes: a **publisher** that sends messages and a **subscriber** that receives and displays them. This exercise will help you understand the basics of ROS2 communication using topics.

Writing Publisher and Subscriber Nodes in Python

Let's begin by creating the publisher and subscriber nodes within your my_robot_pkg.

Step 1: Create the Publisher Node

1. **Navigate to the Python Module Directory:**

bash

```
cd ~/ros2_ws/src/my_robot_pkg/my_robot_pkg
```

2. **Create a New Python File for the Publisher:**

bash

```
touch publisher.py
chmod +x publisher.py
```

3. Edit publisher.py with the Following Content:

```python
#!/usr/bin/env python3
import rclpy
from rclpy.node import Node
from std_msgs.msg import String


class MinimalPublisher(Node):

    def __init__(self):
        super().__init__('minimal_publisher')
        self.publisher_ =
self.create_publisher(String, 'chatter', 10)
        timer_period = 1  # seconds
        self.timer =
self.create_timer(timer_period,
self.timer_callback)
        self.i = 0

    def timer_callback(self):
        msg = String()
        msg.data = f'Hello, ROS2! Count:
{self.i}'
        self.publisher_.publish(msg)
        self.get_logger().info(f'Publishing:
"{msg.data}"')
        self.i += 1
```

```
def main(args=None):
    rclpy.init(args=args)
    minimal_publisher = MinimalPublisher()
    rclpy.spin(minimal_publisher)
    minimal_publisher.destroy_node()
    rclpy.shutdown()


if __name__ == '__main__':
    main()
```

Explanation:

- o **Imports:** Import necessary ROS2 libraries and message types.

- o **MinimalPublisher Class:** Inherits from Node and initializes a publisher on the chatter topic.

- o **timer_callback:** Publishes a String message every second, incrementing a counter.

- o **main Function:** Initializes ROS2, creates the publisher node, and keeps it running.

Step 2: Create the Subscriber Node

1. Create a New Python File for the Subscriber:

```bash
```

```
touch subscriber.py
chmod +x subscriber.py
```

2. Edit subscriber.py with the Following Content:

python

```
#!/usr/bin/env python3
import rclpy
from rclpy.node import Node
from std_msgs.msg import String

class MinimalSubscriber(Node):

    def __init__(self):
        super().__init__('minimal_subscriber')
        self.subscription =
self.create_subscription(
            String,
            'chatter',
            self.listener_callback,
            10)
        self.subscription  # prevent unused
variable warning

    def listener_callback(self, msg):
        self.get_logger().info(f'Received:
"{msg.data}"')

def main(args=None):
    rclpy.init(args=args)
    minimal_subscriber = MinimalSubscriber()
```

```
rclpy.spin(minimal_subscriber)
minimal_subscriber.destroy_node()
rclpy.shutdown()


if __name__ == '__main__':
    main()
```

Explanation:

- o **Imports:** Import necessary ROS2 libraries and message types.

- o **MinimalSubscriber Class:** Inherits from Node and initializes a subscription to the chatter topic.

- o **listener_callback:** Logs the received message.

- o **main Function:** Initializes ROS2, creates the subscriber node, and keeps it running.

Step 3: Update setup.py

To ensure ROS2 recognizes your new scripts, update the setup.py file.

1. **Open setup.py in Your Preferred Editor:**

```bash
```

```
nano ~/ros2_ws/src/my_robot_pkg/setup.py
```

2. **Modify the entry_points Section to Include Your Scripts:**

```python
python

entry_points={
    'console_scripts': [
        'publisher =
my_robot_pkg.publisher:main',
        'subscriber =
my_robot_pkg.subscriber:main',
    ],
},
```

Complete setup.py Example:

```python
python

from setuptools import setup

package_name = 'my_robot_pkg'

setup(
    name=package_name,
    version='0.0.0',
    packages=[package_name],
    data_files=[

('share/ament_index/resource_index/packages',
            ['resource/' + package_name]),
        ('share/' + package_name,
['package.xml']),
    ],
```

```
    install_requires=['setuptools'],
    zip_safe=True,
    maintainer='Your Name',
    maintainer_email='your.email@example.com',
    description='A simple ROS2 package with
publisher and subscriber nodes.',
    license='Apache License 2.0',
    tests_require=['pytest'],
    entry_points={
        'console_scripts': [
            'publisher =
my_robot_pkg.publisher:main',
            'subscriber =
my_robot_pkg.subscriber:main',
        ],
    },
)
```

3. **Save and Exit the Editor.**

Step 4: Build the Package

1. **Navigate to the Workspace Root:**

```bash
```

```bash
cd ~/ros2_ws/
```

2. **Build the Workspace Using Colcon:**

```bash
```

```bash
colcon build
```

3. **Source the Workspace:**

bash

```
source install/setup.bash
```

Step 5: Verify the Nodes

Ensure that ROS2 recognizes your new nodes.

1. **List Available Nodes:**

bash

```
ros2 run my_robot_pkg publisher
ros2 run my_robot_pkg subscriber
```

Expected Behavior:

- o The publisher node starts publishing messages to the chatter topic every second.

- o The subscriber node listens to the chatter topic and logs the received messages.

Publisher and Subscriber Node Interaction Diagram

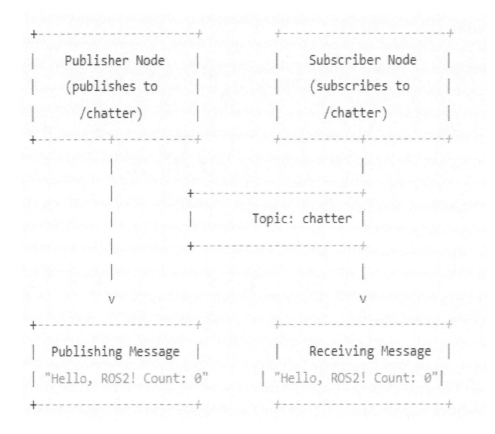

Diagram Explanation: This diagram illustrates the flow of messages from the publisher node to the subscriber node via the chatter topic. The publisher sends a message, which the subscriber receives and logs.

Testing Communication Between Nodes

With both nodes running, it's time to observe the communication in action and troubleshoot any potential issues.

Step 1: Launch the Publisher Node

Open a new terminal, source your workspace, and run the publisher:

```bash
```

```
source ~/ros2_ws/install/setup.bash
ros2 run my_robot_pkg publisher
Expected Output:
```

```csharp
```

```
[INFO] [minimal_publisher]: Publishing: "Hello,
ROS2! Count: 0"
[INFO] [minimal_publisher]: Publishing: "Hello,
ROS2! Count: 1"
[INFO] [minimal_publisher]: Publishing: "Hello,
ROS2! Count: 2"
...
```

Step 2: Launch the Subscriber Node

Open another terminal, source your workspace, and run the subscriber:

```bash
```

```
source ~/ros2_ws/install/setup.bash
ros2 run my_robot_pkg subscriber
```

Expected Output:

```csharp
```

```
[INFO] [minimal_subscriber]: Received: "Hello,
ROS2! Count: 0"
[INFO] [minimal_subscriber]: Received: "Hello,
ROS2! Count: 1"
[INFO] [minimal_subscriber]: Received: "Hello,
ROS2! Count: 2"
...
```

Step 3: Observe the Interaction

- The **publisher** node should continuously send messages with an incrementing count.

- The **subscriber** node should receive and log each message as it's published.

Step 4: Troubleshooting Common Issues

1. **No Messages Received:**

   o **Check Topic Names:** Ensure both nodes are using the exact same topic name (chatter).

   o **Verify Node Status:** Use ros2 node list to see if both nodes are active.

   o **Network Configuration:** If using multiple machines, ensure they are on the same network and ROS_DOMAIN_ID is correctly set.

2. **Messages Not Displaying Correctly:**

   o **Check Message Types:** Ensure both publisher and subscriber are using compatible message types (std_msgs/String).

   o **Review Code:** Look for typos or logical errors in your Python scripts.

3. **High Latency or Dropped Messages:**

   o **QoS Settings:** Adjust Quality of Service parameters if necessary.

   o **System Resources:** Ensure your system has sufficient resources to handle ROS2 processes.

ROS2 Node Communication Testing Steps

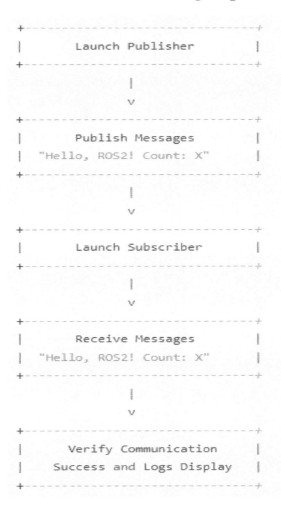

Diagram Explanation: This flowchart outlines the steps to test communication between the publisher and subscriber nodes, ensuring that messages are successfully sent and received.

Conclusion

Congratulations! You've successfully set up ROS2, created your first ROS2 package, and developed simple publisher and subscriber nodes that communicate seamlessly. This hands-on experience has introduced you to the core concepts of ROS2's architecture and communication mechanisms, laying a solid foundation for more complex projects.

Next Steps:

1. **Explore More ROS2 Features:**

   o Dive deeper into topics, services, and actions.

   o Learn about ROS2 parameters, lifecycle management, and launch files.

2. **Integrate Additional Nodes:**

   o Add more nodes to your package to perform diverse tasks.

   o Experiment with different message types and communication patterns.

3. **Advanced Projects:**

   o Move from simple communication to integrating sensors and actuators.

   o Implement autonomous behaviors using feedback from sensors.

4. **Leverage ROS2 Tools:**

- o Utilize RViz for visualization and Gazebo for simulation.

- o Explore ROS2 debugging and monitoring tools to enhance development efficiency.

Remember: *ROS2 is a versatile and powerful framework that empowers you to build sophisticated robotic systems. As you continue your journey, embrace experimentation, seek out community resources, and stay curious. The possibilities with ROS2 and Python are vast, and you're well-equipped to harness their potential.*

You're making great strides in mastering autonomous robotics! Keep pushing forward, and soon you'll be building intelligent systems capable of performing complex, real-world tasks.

Summary

In Chapter 3, "Getting Started with ROS2," we delved into the architecture and communication mechanisms that make ROS2 a cornerstone of modern robotics development. We explored the core concepts of nodes, topics, services, and actions, understanding how they facilitate flexible and scalable communication within robotic systems. Through detailed installation guides for Ubuntu, Windows, and macOS, we ensured that your development environment is set up correctly, laying the groundwork for seamless ROS2 integration.

Creating your first ROS2 package provided hands-on experience with ROS2's structure and build system, reinforcing the theoretical knowledge acquired. The hands-on project of developing simple publisher and subscriber nodes in Python showcased the practical aspects of ROS2 communication, allowing you to observe real-time message exchange and troubleshoot common issues effectively.

This chapter not only equipped you with the essential tools and knowledge to begin your ROS2 journey but also set the stage for more advanced topics and projects. As you continue building on this foundation, ROS2 will empower you to develop sophisticated autonomous robots capable of complex, intelligent behaviors.

Chapter 4: Sensor Integration and Data Processing

Welcome to one of the most exciting and critical aspects of robotics: **Sensor Integration and Data Processing.** Imagine your robot as a living being; sensors are its senses, and data processing is its brain. Without these, a robot would be nothing more than a motorized machine, unable to perceive or interact intelligently with its environment. In this chapter, we'll explore the variety of sensors commonly used in robotics, understand how to integrate them with ROS2, and master the art of processing and visualizing the data they provide. By the end, you'll be equipped to implement a comprehensive sensor suite for your robot, enhancing its autonomy and intelligence.

Common Sensors in Robotics

Sensors are the eyes, ears, and other sensory organs of a robot. They allow robots to perceive their environment, enabling tasks ranging from simple obstacle avoidance to complex decision-making processes. Let's delve into some of the most commonly used sensors in robotics.

LIDAR (Light Detection and Ranging)

LIDAR is a remote sensing technology that measures distances by illuminating targets with laser light and analyzing the reflected light. It's widely used in robotics for mapping, navigation, and obstacle detection.

Key Features:

1. **High Precision:** Offers accurate distance measurements, essential for creating detailed maps.

2. **360-Degree Scanning:** Provides a comprehensive view of the robot's surroundings.

3. **Fast Data Acquisition:** Capable of capturing rapid changes in the environment, crucial for dynamic navigation.

Applications:

- **Autonomous Vehicles:** Enables self-driving cars to detect and navigate around obstacles.

- **Mapping and SLAM:** Assists robots in building and updating maps of their environment.

- **Object Detection:** Identifies and tracks objects in real-time.

LIDAR Functionality Diagram

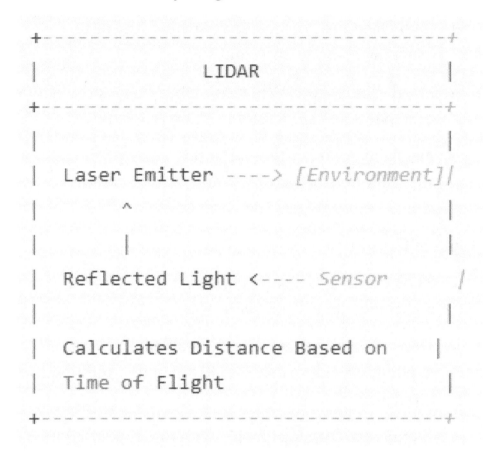

Diagram Explanation: This simple diagram illustrates how LIDAR emits laser beams towards the environment, captures the reflected light, and calculates the distance based on the time it takes for the light to return.

Cameras

Cameras are versatile sensors that capture visual information, enabling tasks like object recognition, visual odometry, and human-robot interaction.

Key Features:

1. **Rich Data:** Provide detailed visual information, including color, texture, and shape.

2. **Depth Perception:** When combined with stereo setups or depth sensors, cameras can perceive depth.

3. **Flexibility:** Can be used for a wide range of applications, from simple vision tasks to complex computer vision algorithms.

Types of Cameras:

- **RGB Cameras:** Capture color images, useful for object recognition and classification.

- **Depth Cameras (e.g., Kinect, RealSense):** Capture depth information, enabling 3D mapping and obstacle avoidance.

- **Monocular Cameras:** Single camera setup, often used in visual odometry and SLAM.

- **Stereo Cameras:** Pair of cameras that provide depth perception through disparity analysis.

Applications:

- **Object Recognition:** Identifying and classifying objects in the environment.

- **Navigation:** Assisting in path planning and obstacle avoidance.

- **Human-Robot Interaction:** Enabling gestures and facial recognition.

IMUs (Inertial Measurement Units)

IMUs are sensors that measure a robot's acceleration and angular velocity, providing crucial data for maintaining balance and orientation.

Key Features:

1. **Motion Detection:** Measures linear acceleration and rotational rates.

2. **Orientation Estimation:** Helps in determining the robot's orientation in space.

3. **Stability Control:** Essential for balancing robots, drones, and humanoid robots.

Applications:

- **Balance and Stability:** Keeps robots upright and stable during movement.

- **Motion Tracking:** Tracks the robot's movement and orientation changes.

- **Navigation:** Assists in dead-reckoning and improving the accuracy of SLAM algorithms.

IMU Data Flow Diagram

```
+----------------------------+
|           IMU              |
+----------------------------+
|                            |
|   +--------------------+  /
|   | Acceleration   |  |
|   | Measurement    |  |
|   +--------------------+  /
|                            |
|            |               |
|   +--------------------+  /
|   | Gyroscope      |  |
|   | Measurement    |  |
|   +--------------------+  /
|            |               |
|   +--------------------+  /
|   | Data Fusion    |  |
|   +--------------------+  /
|            |               |
|   +--------------------+  /
|   | ROS2 Node      |  |
|   | (Orientation)  |  |
|   +--------------------+  /
|                            |
+----------------------------+
```

Diagram Explanation: This diagram outlines how an **IMU** measures acceleration and rotational data, which is then fused and processed by a **ROS2** node to determine the robot's orientation.

Additional Sensors

While LIDAR, cameras, and IMUs are staples in robotics, there are numerous other sensors that enhance a robot's capabilities:

- **Ultrasonic Sensors:** Measure distance using sound waves, useful for simple obstacle detection.

- **Infrared Sensors:** Detect heat signatures and can be used for proximity sensing.

- **Touch Sensors:** Detect physical contact, enabling robots to interact safely with objects and humans.

- **Gas Sensors:** Monitor environmental conditions by detecting specific gases.

- **Temperature and Humidity Sensors:** Track environmental conditions, essential for robots operating in varying climates.

Interfacing Sensors with ROS2

Integrating sensors with ROS2 involves connecting the hardware to the robot and ensuring that ROS2 can effectively communicate with and interpret the sensor data. This section will guide you through the essential steps of interfacing sensors with ROS2, covering sensor drivers, packages, data acquisition, and calibration.

Sensor Drivers and Packages

Sensor drivers are software components that facilitate communication between ROS2 and hardware sensors. They abstract the low-level hardware interactions, allowing developers to work with high-level data streams instead of dealing with complex hardware protocols.

Key Concepts:

1. **Driver Packages:** Pre-built ROS2 packages that provide drivers for specific sensors.

2. **Custom Drivers:** Custom-built drivers when pre-existing ones are unavailable or insufficient.

3. **Message Types:** Define the structure of data exchanged between nodes, ensuring consistency and compatibility.

Popular ROS2 Sensor Packages:

- **LaserScan (LIDAR):** sensor_msgs/LaserScan message type for LIDAR data.

- **Image (Cameras):** sensor_msgs/Image message type for camera images.

- **Imu (IMUs):** sensor_msgs/Imu message type for IMU data.

- **PointCloud2 (3D Sensors):** sensor_msgs/PointCloud2 message type for 3D point clouds.

Example: Installing a LIDAR Driver Package

bash

```
sudo apt install ros-humble-rplidar-ros
```

Explanation: This command installs the ROS2 driver package for **RPLIDAR**, a popular LIDAR sensor. Replace rplidar-ros with the appropriate package name for different LIDAR models.

Data Acquisition and Calibration

Data Acquisition involves collecting data from sensors and making it available for processing within ROS2. **Calibration** ensures that the sensor data is accurate and reliable, correcting any inherent biases or errors.

Data Acquisition

1. **Connect the Sensor Hardware:**

   o Physically connect the sensor to the robot's mainboard (e.g., Raspberry Pi, Arduino).

   o Ensure secure and correct wiring to prevent data loss or hardware damage.

2. **Launch the Sensor Driver:**

   o Use ROS2 launch files or command-line tools to start the sensor driver node.

Example: Launching LIDAR Driver

```bash
```

```
ros2 launch rplidar_ros rplidar.launch.py
```

3. **Verify Data Streams:**

   o Use ROS2 command-line tools to inspect active topics and ensure data is being published.

```bash
```

```
ros2 topic list
ros2 topic echo /scan
```

4. **Integrate with Other Nodes:**

   o Connect sensor data to processing nodes, such as mapping or navigation modules.

Example: Feeding LIDAR data into a SLAM node for real-time mapping.

Calibration

1. **Understand Calibration Requirements:**

   o Different sensors have unique calibration needs. For instance, cameras require intrinsic and extrinsic calibration, while IMUs may need bias correction.

2. Use **ROS2 Calibration Tools:**

- o ROS2 offers specialized tools for calibrating various sensors.

Example: Camera Calibration using camera_calibration Package

```bash


ros2 run camera_calibration cameracalibrator.py --size 8x6 --square 0.025 image:=/camera/image
```

3. **Perform Calibration Procedures:**

- o Follow the calibration process specific to the sensor, which typically involves moving the sensor through specific motions or capturing images of calibration patterns.

4. **Validate Calibration:**

- o After calibration, verify the accuracy of sensor data through testing and visualization.

Example: Check if the camera images are free from distortion and accurately represent the environment.

Sensor Calibration Workflow Diagram

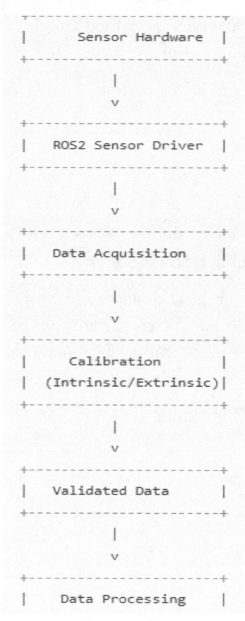

Diagram Explanation: This workflow diagram outlines the process from sensor hardware connection to validated data ready for processing, emphasizing the importance of calibration in ensuring data accuracy.

Hands-On Project: Implementing a Sensor Suite

Building a sensor suite equips your robot with the ability to perceive and interact intelligently with its environment. In this hands-on project, we'll integrate a combination of LIDAR, camera, and IMU sensors into your robot, process the incoming data, and visualize it using ROS2 tools.

Connecting Sensors to Your Robot

Objective: Equip your robot with LIDAR, camera, and IMU sensors, ensuring seamless communication with ROS2.

Components Needed:

1. **LIDAR Sensor:** e.g., RPLIDAR A1

2. **Camera Module:** e.g., Raspberry Pi Camera Module V2

3. **IMU Sensor:** e.g., MPU-9250

4. **ROS2-Compatible Hardware Interface:** e.g., Raspberry Pi 4

5. **Wiring and Connectors:** Jumper wires, USB cables

6. **Power Supply:** Sufficient to power all sensors and the mainboard

Step-by-Step Connection:

Step 1: Mounting the Sensors

1. **LIDAR Sensor:**

   - Secure the LIDAR on the robot chassis, ensuring it has an unobstructed 360-degree view.

   - Use mounting brackets or adhesive tape for stability.

2. **Camera Module:**

   - Attach the camera to the front of the robot for a clear field of view.

   - Ensure the camera is securely mounted to prevent vibrations.

3. **IMU Sensor:**

   - Mount the IMU close to the robot's center of gravity for accurate motion tracking.

   - Orient the IMU according to the manufacturer's guidelines.

Step 2: Wiring the Sensors

1. **LIDAR:**

   - Connect the LIDAR's USB port to the Raspberry Pi.

   - Ensure proper power supply connections if not USB-powered.

2. **Camera:**

- o Connect the camera to the Raspberry Pi's dedicated camera interface.

- o Secure the ribbon cable to prevent disconnection.

3. **IMU:**

- o Connect the IMU to the Raspberry Pi via I2C or SPI, depending on the sensor's interface.

- o Use jumper wires to connect the SDA, SCL (for I2C) or MOSI, MISO, SCLK, CS (for SPI), along with power and ground.

Step 3: Power Management

1. **Ensure Adequate Power Supply:**

- o Verify that the power supply can handle the combined current draw of all sensors and the Raspberry Pi.

- o Use a regulated power source to prevent voltage fluctuations that could damage components.

2. **Implement Power Switching (Optional):**

- o For advanced setups, consider integrating power switching mechanisms to control sensor power states programmatically.

Safety Tip: Always disconnect power before making or modifying connections to prevent short circuits and hardware damage.

Processing and Visualizing Sensor Data

Objective: Develop ROS2 nodes to process incoming sensor data and visualize it using ROS2 tools like RViz and Gazebo.

Step 1: Processing LIDAR Data

1. **Launch the LIDAR Driver:**

bash

```
ros2 launch rplidar_ros rplidar.launch.py
```

2. **Create a ROS2 Node for LIDAR Data Processing:**

   - **Node Functionality:** Subscribes to the LIDAR data topic, processes the scan data, and publishes processed information for navigation.

   - **Example Implementation:**

python

```python
# lidar_processor.py
import rclpy
from rclpy.node import Node
from sensor_msgs.msg import LaserScan
import math

class LidarProcessor(Node):
    def __init__(self):
        super().__init__('lidar_processor')
```

```
        self.subscription =
self.create_subscription(
            LaserScan,
            '/scan',
            self.lidar_callback,
            10)
        self.publisher_ =
self.create_publisher(String, 'processed_lidar',
10)


    def lidar_callback(self, msg):
        # Example: Find the minimum distance
        min_distance = min(msg.ranges)
        angle = msg.ranges.index(min_distance) *
msg.angle_increment
        self.get_logger().info(f'Min Distance:
{min_distance} at Angle: {math.degrees(angle)}')
        # Publish processed data if needed
        # processed_msg = String()
        # processed_msg.data =
f'{min_distance},{math.degrees(angle)}'
        # self.publisher_.publish(processed_msg)

def main(args=None):
    rclpy.init(args=args)
    lidar_processor = LidarProcessor()
    rclpy.spin(lidar_processor)
    lidar_processor.destroy_node()
```

```python
rclpy.shutdown()


if __name__ == '__main__':
    main()
```

3. Add the Node to Your ROS2 Package:

- ○ **Update setup.py:**

```python
python


entry_points={
    'console_scripts': [
        'publisher =
my_robot_pkg.publisher:main',
        'subscriber =
my_robot_pkg.subscriber:main',
        'lidar_processor =
my_robot_pkg.lidar_processor:main',
    ],
},
```

4. Build the Package:

```bash
bash


cd ~/ros2_ws/
colcon build
source install/setup.bash
```

5. **Run the LIDAR Processor Node:**

bash

```
ros2 run my_robot_pkg lidar_processor
```

Step 2: Processing Camera Data

1. **Launch the Camera Driver:**

bash

```
ros2 run usb_cam usb_cam_node_exe
```

2. **Create a ROS2 Node for Camera Data Processing:**

   o **Node Functionality:** Subscribes to the camera image topic, performs image processing (e.g., edge detection), and publishes the processed images.

   o **Example Implementation:**

python

```python
# camera_processor.py
import rclpy
from rclpy.node import Node
from sensor_msgs.msg import Image
from cv_bridge import CvBridge
import cv2

class CameraProcessor(Node):
    def __init__(self):
```

```
        super().__init__('camera_processor')
        self.subscription =
self.create_subscription(
            Image,
            '/usb_cam/image_raw',
            self.image_callback,
            10)
        self.publisher_ =
self.create_publisher(Image, '/camera/processed',
10)
        self.bridge = CvBridge()


    def image_callback(self, msg):
        cv_image = self.bridge.imgmsg_to_cv2(msg,
desired_encoding='bgr8')
        gray = cv2.cvtColor(cv_image,
cv2.COLOR_BGR2GRAY)
        edges = cv2.Canny(gray, 100, 200)
        processed_image =
self.bridge.cv2_to_imgmsg(edges,
encoding='mono8')
        self.publisher_.publish(processed_image)
        self.get_logger().info('Processed image
and published edges.')


def main(args=None):
    rclpy.init(args=args)
    camera_processor = CameraProcessor()
```

```
rclpy.spin(camera_processor)
camera_processor.destroy_node()
rclpy.shutdown()


if __name__ == '__main__':
    main()
```

3. Install cv_bridge:

```bash
sudo apt install ros-humble-cv-bridge
```

4. Add the Node to Your ROS2 Package:

- #### Update setup.py:

```python
entry_points={
    'console_scripts': [
        'publisher =
my_robot_pkg.publisher:main',
        'subscriber =
my_robot_pkg.subscriber:main',
        'lidar_processor =
my_robot_pkg.lidar_processor:main',
        'camera_processor =
my_robot_pkg.camera_processor:main',
    ],
},
```

5. Build the Package:

bash

```
cd ~/ros2_ws/
colcon build
source install/setup.bash
```

6. Run the Camera Processor Node:

bash

```
ros2 run my_robot_pkg camera_processor
```

Step 3: Processing IMU Data

1. Launch the IMU Driver:

bash

```
ros2 run mpu9250_ros mpu9250_node
```

2. Create a ROS2 Node for IMU Data Processing:

- o **Node Functionality:** Subscribes to the IMU data topic, calculates orientation, and publishes processed orientation data.

- o **Example Implementation:**

python

```
# imu_processor.py
import rclpy
from rclpy.node import Node
```

```python
from sensor_msgs.msg import Imu
import math


class ImuProcessor(Node):
    def __init__(self):
        super().__init__('imu_processor')
        self.subscription = self.create_subscription(
            Imu,
            '/imu/data',
            self.imu_callback,
            10)
        self.publisher_ = self.create_publisher(String, 'processed_imu', 10)


    def imu_callback(self, msg):
        # Example: Calculate roll and pitch from quaternion
        q = msg.orientation
        sinr_cosp = 2 * (q.w * q.x + q.y * q.z)
        cosr_cosp = 1 - 2 * (q.x * q.x + q.y * q.y)
        roll = math.atan2(sinr_cosp, cosr_cosp)

        sinp = 2 * (q.w * q.y - q.z * q.x)
        if abs(sinp) >= 1:
```

```python
            pitch = math.sign(math.pi / 2, sinp)
# use 90 degrees if out of range
        else:
            pitch = math.asin(sinp)


        self.get_logger().info(f'Roll:
{math.degrees(roll)}, Pitch:
{math.degrees(pitch)}')
        # Publish processed data if needed
        # processed_msg = String()
        # processed_msg.data = f'{roll},{pitch}'
        # self.publisher_.publish(processed_msg)


def main(args=None):
    rclpy.init(args=args)
    imu_processor = ImuProcessor()
    rclpy.spin(imu_processor)
    imu_processor.destroy_node()
    rclpy.shutdown()


if __name__ == '__main__':
    main()
```

3. Add the Node to Your ROS2 Package:

- #### Update setup.py:

```python


entry_points={
```

```
    'console_scripts': [
         'publisher =
my_robot_pkg.publisher:main',
         'subscriber =
my_robot_pkg.subscriber:main',
         'lidar_processor =
my_robot_pkg.lidar_processor:main',
         'camera_processor =
my_robot_pkg.camera_processor:main',
         'imu_processor =
my_robot_pkg.imu_processor:main',
    ],
},
```

4. Build the Package:

```bash
```

```bash
cd ~/ros2_ws/
colcon build
source install/setup.bash
```

5. Run the IMU Processor Node:

```bash
```

```bash
ros2 run my_robot_pkg imu_processor
```

Sensor Data Processing Flowchart

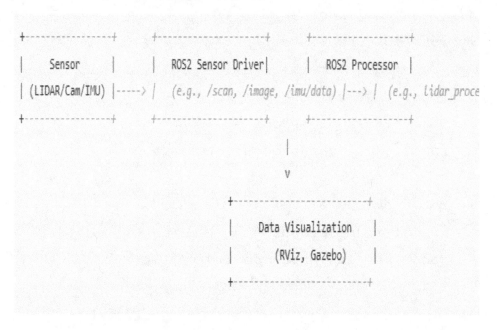

Diagram Explanation: This flowchart demonstrates how sensor data flows from the hardware through ROS2 sensor drivers, is processed by dedicated ROS2 nodes, and finally visualized using ROS2 tools like RViz and Gazebo.

Calibrating Sensors for Accurate Data

Accurate sensor data is paramount for reliable robot performance. Calibration corrects any inherent biases or errors in sensor measurements, ensuring that the data reflects the true state of the environment.

Calibration Steps for Common Sensors

1. **LIDAR Calibration:**

   o **Check Alignment:** Ensure the LIDAR is correctly mounted and aligned with the robot's frame.

   o **Environmental Calibration:** Perform scans in a known environment to verify distance measurements.

   o **Software Calibration:** Use ROS2 packages to fine-tune parameters like scan rate and angle range.

2. **Camera Calibration:**

   o **Intrinsic Calibration:** Correct lens distortions and define camera parameters (focal length, principal point).

   o **Extrinsic Calibration:** Define the camera's position and orientation relative to the robot's frame.

   o **ROS2 Tools:** Utilize packages like camera_calibration to automate the calibration process.

3. **IMU Calibration:**

   o **Bias Correction:** Remove any constant bias in accelerometer and gyroscope readings.

- o **Orientation Calibration:** Ensure the IMU's orientation matches the robot's frame.

- o **Calibration Procedures:** Follow manufacturer guidelines or use ROS2 calibration packages for accurate calibration.

Conclusion

Integrating sensors and processing their data is a cornerstone of autonomous robotics. By equipping your robot with a comprehensive sensor suite, you enable it to perceive and interact intelligently with its environment. Through careful integration and calibration, you ensure that the data your robot relies on is accurate and reliable, laying the foundation for advanced functionalities like autonomous navigation and decision-making.

Next Steps:

1. **Expand Your Sensor Suite:**

   - o Incorporate additional sensors such as infrared, gas, or tactile sensors to enhance your robot's perception.

   - o Experiment with different sensor combinations to achieve desired capabilities.

2. **Advanced Data Processing:**

   - o Implement more sophisticated algorithms for sensor fusion, allowing your robot to make informed decisions based on multiple data sources.

- ○ Explore machine learning techniques to interpret sensor data and predict environmental changes.

3. **Real-World Testing:**

- ○ Deploy your sensor-integrated robot in various environments to test its perception and interaction capabilities.

- ○ Use **ROS2** visualization tools like **RViz** to monitor sensor data in real-time and make necessary adjustments.

4. **Optimize Performance:**

- ○ Fine-tune sensor parameters and processing algorithms to enhance performance and responsiveness.

- ○ Implement strategies for managing sensor data efficiently, especially in resource-constrained systems.

Remember: *The effectiveness of your robot largely depends on the quality and integration of its sensors. Investing time in understanding and mastering sensor integration and data processing will pay dividends in creating intelligent, autonomous systems capable of tackling complex real-world challenges.*

You're on the path to building sophisticated, perceptive robots! Embrace the complexities, experiment with different sensor setups, and continue pushing the boundaries of what's possible in autonomous robotics.

Summary

In Chapter 4, "Sensor Integration and Data Processing," we delved into the essential role sensors play in empowering robots to perceive and interact with their environment. We explored a variety of common sensors, including LIDAR, cameras, and IMUs, understanding their functionalities and applications in robotics. The chapter detailed the process of interfacing these sensors with ROS2, highlighting the importance of sensor drivers, packages, and robust data acquisition methods. Calibration techniques were discussed to ensure the accuracy and reliability of sensor data, a crucial aspect for effective robot performance.

Through a comprehensive hands-on project, we implemented a sensor suite by integrating LIDAR, camera, and IMU sensors into a robot, developing ROS2 nodes to process and visualize the incoming data. This practical experience reinforced the theoretical concepts, providing a solid foundation for more advanced sensor integrations and data processing techniques.

By mastering sensor integration and data processing, you equip your robots with the senses and cognitive abilities necessary for autonomous operation, paving the way for sophisticated behaviors and intelligent interactions in real-world scenarios.

Chapter 5: Actuator Control and Motor Management

Welcome to the dynamic world of **Actuator Control and Motor Management!** Imagine your robot as a living creature—its actuators are its muscles, enabling movement and interaction with the environment. Just as our muscles contract and relax to perform actions, actuators in robots convert electrical signals into physical motions. Mastering actuator control is pivotal for creating responsive, precise, and versatile robotic systems. In this chapter, we'll explore the various types of actuators, delve into controlling them using ROS2 and Python, understand the nuances of PWM control and motor drivers, and implement feedback mechanisms for precision. To solidify your understanding, we'll embark on a hands-on project focused on advanced motor control, integrating speed and position management alongside actuator feedback within ROS2. Let's power up and get moving!

Types of Actuators

Before diving into the intricacies of controlling actuators, it's essential to understand the different types available. Think of actuators as the engines of your robot, each suited for specific tasks based on their unique characteristics.

DC Motors

DC Motors are the workhorses of robotics, renowned for their simplicity and versatility.

Key Features:

1. **Continuous Rotation:** DC motors can rotate indefinitely, making them ideal for applications requiring continuous motion.

2. **Speed Control:** Easily adjustable speed through voltage or PWM (Pulse Width Modulation) control.

3. **Torque Production:** Capable of generating significant torque, especially when paired with appropriate gearing.

Applications:

- **Wheeled Robots:** Driving the wheels to propel the robot forward or backward.

- **Industrial Robots:** Powering conveyor belts and other linear motion systems.

- **DIY Projects:** Foundational component in many hobbyist robotic builds.

DC Motor Diagram

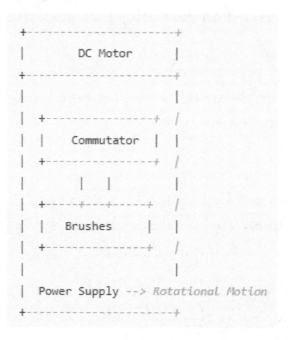

Diagram Explanation: This diagram showcases the internal components of a DC motor. Electrical energy is supplied to the motor, causing the brushes to transfer current to the commutator, which in turn generates rotational motion.

Servos

Servos are specialized actuators designed for precise control over angular or linear position.

Key Features:

1. **Positional Control:** Capable of moving to and maintaining a specific position.

2. **Feedback Mechanism:** Equipped with internal sensors (typically potentiometers) to monitor and adjust position.

3. **Compact Design:** Ideal for applications with space constraints.

Applications:

- **Robotic Arms:** Controlling the precise movement of joints.

- **RC Vehicles:** Steering mechanisms in remote-controlled cars and boats.

- **Camera Gimbals:** Stabilizing cameras to maintain steady footage.

Servo Mechanism Diagram

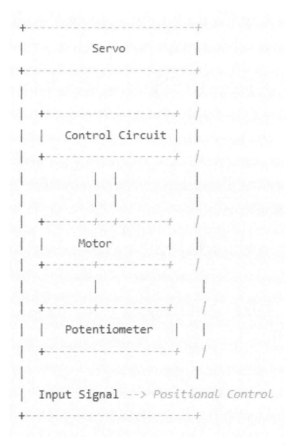

Diagram Explanation: This diagram illustrates the internal structure of a servo. An input signal directs the control circuit, which adjusts the motor's position based on feedback from the potentiometer, ensuring precise positional control.

Stepper Motors

Stepper Motors offer precise control over rotation, moving in discrete steps rather than continuous motion.

Key Features:

1. **Incremental Steps:** Rotate in fixed angle increments, allowing for exact positioning.

2. **Open-Loop Control:** Often operated without feedback, relying on step counts for position accuracy.

3. **High Torque at Low Speeds:** Suitable for applications requiring strong holding torque.

Applications:

- **3D Printers:** Precise movement of print heads and build platforms.

- **CNC Machines:** Controlling tool positions with high accuracy.

- **Automated Door Openers:** Ensuring consistent and repeatable opening mechanisms.

Controlling Actuators with ROS2 and Python

Now that you're familiar with the types of actuators, let's explore how to control them using ROS2 and Python. ROS2 provides a robust framework for managing actuator behavior, while Python offers the flexibility and simplicity needed for effective control.

PWM Control and Motor Drivers

Pulse Width Modulation (PWM) is a technique used to control the power delivered to actuators, allowing for smooth and precise adjustments in speed and position.

Why PWM?

- **Efficiency:** Reduces power loss by controlling voltage levels without dissipating excess energy as heat.

- **Precision:** Fine-tunes actuator behavior by varying the duty cycle of the PWM signal.

- **Compatibility:** Widely supported by motor drivers and microcontrollers.

Motor Drivers:

Motor drivers act as intermediaries between the ROS2-controlled microcontroller and the actuators, managing the power and direction of motor operations.

Common Motor Drivers:

1. **L298N Dual H-Bridge Motor Driver:**

   o Controls two DC motors independently.

   o Handles direction and speed via PWM signals.

2. **TB6612FNG Dual Motor Driver:**

   o More efficient than L298N with lower voltage drops.

   o Controls two DC motors or one stepper motor.

3. **Servo Controllers:**

   o Designed specifically for controlling servo motors.

   o Often provide dedicated PWM channels for precise positional control.

Step-by-Step PWM Control with ROS2 and Python:

Step 1: Connect the Motor Driver to the Microcontroller

1. **Power Connections:**

   o Connect the motor driver's VCC and GND to the power supply.

   o Ensure that the power supply matches the motor driver's voltage requirements.

2. **Control Pins:**

- o Connect the PWM input pins from the motor driver to the GPIO pins on the microcontroller (e.g., Raspberry Pi).

Step 2: Install Necessary ROS2 Packages

Ensure that you have the rclpy and gpiozero libraries installed for Python-based ROS2 node development.

bash

```
sudo apt install python3-gpiozero
pip3 install rclpy
```

Step 3: Write a ROS2 Python Node to Control the Motor

Create a new Python script within your ROS2 package to manage motor speed and direction.

python

```
# motor_control.py
import rclpy
from rclpy.node import Node
from gpiozero import PWMOutputDevice
from std_msgs.msg import Int32

class MotorController(Node):
    def __init__(self):
        super().__init__('motor_controller')
        # Initialize PWM channels
```

```python
        self.pwm_left = PWMOutputDevice(pin=18)
# GPIO18 for left motor
        self.pwm_right = PWMOutputDevice(pin=19)
# GPIO19 for right motor
        # Subscriber to motor speed commands
        self.subscription =
self.create_subscription(
            Int32,
            'motor_speed',
            self.speed_callback,
            10)
        self.get_logger().info('Motor Controller
Node Initialized.')

    def speed_callback(self, msg):
        speed = msg.data
        # Map speed value to PWM duty cycle (0.0
to 1.0)
        duty_cycle = max(0.0, min(1.0, speed /
100.0))
        self.pwm_left.value = duty_cycle
        self.pwm_right.value = duty_cycle
        self.get_logger().info(f'Setting motor
speed to {speed}% (Duty Cycle: {duty_cycle})')

def main(args=None):
    rclpy.init(args=args)
    motor_controller = MotorController()
```

```
    rclpy.spin(motor_controller)
    motor_controller.destroy_node()
    rclpy.shutdown()


if __name__ == '__main__':
    main()
```

Explanation:

- **PWMOutputDevice:** Utilizes the gpiozero library to control PWM signals on specified GPIO pins.

- **Subscription:** Listens to the motor_speed topic for speed commands.

- **Duty Cycle Mapping:** Converts speed percentage to a PWM duty cycle between 0.0 and 1.0.

- **Logging:** Provides real-time feedback on motor speed settings.

Step 4: Update setup.py to Include the Motor Control Node

```python

entry_points={
    'console_scripts': [
        'publisher =
my_robot_pkg.publisher:main',
        'subscriber =
my_robot_pkg.subscriber:main',
        'lidar_processor =
my_robot_pkg.lidar_processor:main',
```

```
        'camera_processor =
my_robot_pkg.camera_processor:main',
        'imu_processor =
my_robot_pkg.imu_processor:main',
        'motor_control =
my_robot_pkg.motor_control:main',
    ],
},
```

Step 5: Build and Source the Workspace

bash

```
cd ~/ros2_ws/
colcon build
source install/setup.bash
```

Step 6: Run the Motor Control Node

bash

```
ros2 run my_robot_pkg motor_control
```

Expected Output:

css

```
[INFO] [motor_controller]: Motor Controller Node
Initialized.
```

Feedback Mechanisms for Precision Control

To achieve precise control over actuators, incorporating feedback mechanisms is essential. Feedback allows the system to monitor and adjust actuator behavior in real-time, ensuring accuracy and responsiveness.

Types of Feedback Mechanisms:

1. **Encoders:**

   o **Rotary Encoders:** Attached to motors to measure rotational position and speed.

   o **Linear Encoders:** Measure linear movement, useful for applications like robotic arms.

2. **Potentiometers:**

   o Integrated into servo motors to provide position feedback.

   o Allows for precise positional control by monitoring angular displacement.

3. **IMUs (Inertial Measurement Units):**

   o Provide orientation and motion data.

   o Useful for balancing robots and stabilizing platforms.

Implementing Feedback for Precision:

Step 1: Attach Encoders to the Motors

1. **Mount Rotary Encoders:** Securely attach encoders to the motor shafts.

2. **Connect Encoder Outputs:** Wire the encoder signals to the microcontroller's GPIO pins capable of handling interrupts.

Step 2: Modify the ROS2 Motor Controller Node to Incorporate Feedback

Enhance the motor_control.py script to read encoder data and adjust motor commands accordingly.

python

```python
# motor_control_with_feedback.py
import rclpy
from rclpy.node import Node
from gpiozero import PWMOutputDevice,
DigitalInputDevice
from std_msgs.msg import Int32
import time

class MotorController(Node):
    def __init__(self):
        super().__init__('motor_controller')
        # Initialize PWM channels
        self.pwm_left = PWMOutputDevice(pin=18)
```

```python
        self.pwm_right = PWMOutputDevice(pin=19)
        # Initialize encoders
        self.encoder_left =
DigitalInputDevice(pin=20)
        self.encoder_right =
DigitalInputDevice(pin=21)
        self.left_count = 0
        self.right_count = 0
        # Subscriber to motor speed commands
        self.subscription =
self.create_subscription(
            Int32,
            'motor_speed',
            self.speed_callback,
            10)
        # Timer for feedback processing
        self.timer = self.create_timer(0.1,
self.feedback_callback)
        self.get_logger().info('Motor Controller
with Feedback Node Initialized.')

    def speed_callback(self, msg):
        speed = msg.data
        duty_cycle = max(0.0, min(1.0, speed /
100.0))
        self.pwm_left.value = duty_cycle
        self.pwm_right.value = duty_cycle
```

```
        self.get_logger().info(f'Setting motor
speed to {speed}% (Duty Cycle: {duty_cycle})')


    def feedback_callback(self):
        # Read encoder states
        left_state = self.encoder_left.value
        right_state = self.encoder_right.value
        # Simple count increment (for
demonstration)
        if left_state:
            self.left_count += 1
        if right_state:
            self.right_count += 1
        # Log encoder counts
        self.get_logger().info(f'Left Encoder
Count: {self.left_count}, Right Encoder Count:
{self.right_count}')


def main(args=None):
    rclpy.init(args=args)
    motor_controller = MotorController()
    rclpy.spin(motor_controller)
    motor_controller.destroy_node()
    rclpy.shutdown()


if __name__ == '__main__':
    main()
```

Explanation:

- **DigitalInputDevice:** Uses gpiozero to monitor encoder pins.

- **Encoder Counts:** Tracks the number of pulses received, indicating rotation.

- **Feedback Callback:** Periodically reads encoder states and updates counts.

- **Logging:** Provides real-time feedback on encoder counts, enabling monitoring of motor performance.

Step 3: Update setup.py and Build the Package

python

```python
entry_points={
    'console_scripts': [
        'publisher =
my_robot_pkg.publisher:main',
        'subscriber =
my_robot_pkg.subscriber:main',
        'lidar_processor =
my_robot_pkg.lidar_processor:main',
        'camera_processor =
my_robot_pkg.camera_processor:main',
        'imu_processor =
my_robot_pkg.imu_processor:main',
        'motor_control =
my_robot_pkg.motor_control:main',
```

```
      'motor_control_feedback =
my_robot_pkg.motor_control_with_feedback:main',
    ],
},
bash

cd ~/ros2_ws/
colcon build
source install/setup.bash
```

Step 4: Run the Enhanced Motor Control Node

```
bash

ros2 run my_robot_pkg motor_control_feedback
```

Expected Output:

```
less

[INFO] [motor_controller]: Motor Controller with
Feedback Node Initialized.
[INFO] [motor_controller]: Setting motor speed to
50% (Duty Cycle: 0.5)
[INFO] [motor_controller]: Left Encoder Count:
10, Right Encoder Count: 12

...
```

Note: The encoder counts will increment based on motor rotations, providing real-time feedback on motor performance.

Hands-On Project: Advanced Motor Control

Ready to take your motor control skills to the next level? In this hands-on project, we'll implement advanced motor control techniques, focusing on speed and position management while integrating actuator feedback within ROS2. This project will enhance your robot's precision and responsiveness, enabling it to perform more complex tasks with greater accuracy.

Implementing Speed and Position Control

Objective: Develop a ROS2 node that controls motor speed and position using PWM signals and encoder feedback, achieving precise and responsive motor behavior.

Components Needed:

1. **DC Motors with Encoders:** Motors equipped with rotary encoders for feedback.

2. **Motor Driver:** e.g., L298N Dual H-Bridge Motor Driver.

3. **Microcontroller:** e.g., Raspberry Pi 4.

4. **Power Supply:** Appropriate for motors and microcontroller.

5. **Wiring and Connectors:** Jumper wires, breadboard.

6. **ROS2 Packages:** rclpy, gpiozero, std_msgs.

Step-by-Step Implementation:

Step 1: Connect the Hardware

1. **Mount the DC Motors with Encoders:**

   o Secure the motors to the robot chassis.

   o Ensure encoders are firmly attached to prevent miscounts.

2. **Wire the Motor Driver to the Microcontroller:**

   o **Power Connections:**

      ▪ Connect the motor driver's VCC and GND to the power supply.

      ▪ Ensure voltage levels match motor specifications.

   o **Control Pins:**

      ▪ Connect PWM input pins (e.g., IN1, IN2 for direction) to GPIO pins on the Raspberry Pi.

      ▪ Connect encoder outputs to designated GPIO pins for feedback.

3. **Ensure Proper Power Management:**

o Verify all connections are secure.

o Double-check polarity to prevent damage.

Step 2: Develop the ROS2 Node for Speed Control

Create a Python script to manage motor speed using PWM signals.

python

```python
# speed_control.py
import rclpy
from rclpy.node import Node
from std_msgs.msg import Int32
from gpiozero import PWMOutputDevice
import time

class SpeedController(Node):
    def __init__(self):
        super().__init__('speed_controller')
        # Initialize PWM channels for left and right motors
        self.pwm_left = PWMOutputDevice(pin=18)
        self.pwm_right = PWMOutputDevice(pin=19)
        # Subscriber to speed commands
        self.subscription = self.create_subscription(
            Int32,
            'motor_speed',
            self.speed_callback,
```

```
            10)
        self.get_logger().info('Speed Controller
Node Initialized.')


    def speed_callback(self, msg):
        speed = msg.data
        # Map speed percentage to PWM duty cycle
(0.0 to 1.0)
        duty_cycle = max(0.0, min(1.0, speed /
100.0))
        self.pwm_left.value = duty_cycle
        self.pwm_right.value = duty_cycle
        self.get_logger().info(f'Setting motor
speed to {speed}% (Duty Cycle: {duty_cycle})')


def main(args=None):
    rclpy.init(args=args)
    speed_controller = SpeedController()
    rclpy.spin(speed_controller)
    speed_controller.destroy_node()
    rclpy.shutdown()


if __name__ == '__main__':
    main()
```

Explanation:

- **PWMOutputDevice:** Controls the duty cycle of the PWM signals for motor speed regulation.

- **Subscriber:** Listens to the motor_speed topic for speed percentage commands.

- **Duty Cycle Mapping:** Converts speed percentage to a PWM value between 0.0 and 1.0.

Step 3: Develop the ROS2 Node for Position Control

Create a Python script that controls motor position using encoder feedback.

python

```python
# position_control.py
import rclpy
from rclpy.node import Node
from std_msgs.msg import Int32
from gpiozero import PWMOutputDevice,
DigitalInputDevice
import time

class PositionController(Node):
    def __init__(self):
        super().__init__('position_controller')
        # Initialize PWM channels
        self.pwm_left = PWMOutputDevice(pin=18)
        self.pwm_right = PWMOutputDevice(pin=19)
        # Initialize encoders
        self.encoder_left =
DigitalInputDevice(pin=20)
```

```python
        self.encoder_right =
DigitalInputDevice(pin=21)
        self.left_count = 0
        self.right_count = 0
        # Subscriber to position commands
        self.subscription =
self.create_subscription(
            Int32,
            'motor_position',
            self.position_callback,
            10)
        # Timer for feedback processing
        self.timer = self.create_timer(0.1,
self.feedback_callback)
        self.target_position = 0
        self.get_logger().info('Position
Controller Node Initialized.')

    def position_callback(self, msg):
        self.target_position = msg.data
        self.get_logger().info(f'Setting target
position to {self.target_position} steps.')
        self.move_to_position()

    def move_to_position(self):
        while self.left_count <
self.target_position and self.right_count <
self.target_position:
```

```python
            self.pwm_left.value = 0.5  # Set
speed (50%)
            self.pwm_right.value = 0.5
            time.sleep(0.1)
        self.stop()


    def feedback_callback(self):
        # Read encoder states
        if self.encoder_left.value:
            self.left_count += 1
        if self.encoder_right.value:
            self.right_count += 1
        # Log encoder counts
        self.get_logger().info(f'Left Encoder:
{self.left_count}, Right Encoder:
{self.right_count}')


    def stop(self):
        self.pwm_left.value = 0.0
        self.pwm_right.value = 0.0
        self.get_logger().info('Reached target
position. Motors stopped.')

def main(args=None):
    rclpy.init(args=args)
    position_controller = PositionController()
    rclpy.spin(position_controller)
    position_controller.destroy_node()
```

```
    rclpy.shutdown()


if __name__ == '__main__':
    main()
```

Explanation:

- **Position Command:** Listens to the motor_position topic for target step counts.

- **Motor Control:** Runs motors at 50% speed until encoder counts reach the target.

- **Feedback:** Continuously monitors encoder counts to determine when to stop motors.

Step 4: Update setup.py to Include New Nodes

```python
entry_points={
    'console_scripts': [
        'publisher =
my_robot_pkg.publisher:main',
        'subscriber =
my_robot_pkg.subscriber:main',
        'lidar_processor =
my_robot_pkg.lidar_processor:main',
        'camera_processor =
my_robot_pkg.camera_processor:main',
        'imu_processor =
my_robot_pkg.imu_processor:main',
```

```
        'motor_control =
my_robot_pkg.motor_control:main',
        'motor_control_feedback =
my_robot_pkg.motor_control_with_feedback:main',
        'speed_control =
my_robot_pkg.speed_control:main',
        'position_control =
my_robot_pkg.position_control:main',
    ],
},
```

Step 5: Build and Source the Workspace

```bash
cd ~/ros2_ws/
colcon build
source install/setup.bash
```

Step 6: Run the Speed and Position Control Nodes

1. Run Speed Control Node:

```bash
ros2 run my_robot_pkg speed_control
```

2. Run Position Control Node:

```bash
ros2 run my_robot_pkg position_control
```

Step 7: Send Speed and Position Commands

Use ROS2 command-line tools or create publisher nodes to send commands to the motor_speed and motor_position topics.

bash

```
# Sending speed command
ros2 topic pub /motor_speed std_msgs/Int32 "data:
75"  # Sets speed to 75%

# Sending position command
ros2 topic pub /motor_position std_msgs/Int32
"data: 1000"  # Moves motors 1000 steps
```

Expected Output:

less

```
[INFO] [speed_controller]: Setting motor speed to
75% (Duty Cycle: 0.75)
[INFO] [position_controller]: Setting target
position to 1000 steps.
[INFO] [position_controller]: Left Encoder: 1,
Right Encoder: 1
...
[INFO] [position_controller]: Reached target
position. Motors stopped.
```

Integrating Actuator Feedback into ROS2

Feedback integration is crucial for achieving precise and reliable actuator control. By incorporating feedback mechanisms, you enable your robot to adjust its actions based on real-time data, enhancing performance and adaptability.

Benefits of Feedback Integration:

1. **Precision Control:** Achieves exact positioning and speed adjustments.

2. **Error Correction:** Detects and compensates for discrepancies between desired and actual actuator states.

3. **Enhanced Responsiveness:** Adapts to dynamic environments and changing conditions.

Step-by-Step Integration:

Step 1: Implement Encoder Feedback in ROS2 Nodes

Ensure that your ROS2 nodes correctly interpret encoder data to monitor motor performance.

Example: Enhanced Position Control Node

```python

# enhanced_position_control.py
import rclpy
from rclpy.node import Node
```

```python
from std_msgs.msg import Int32
from gpiozero import PWMOutputDevice,
DigitalInputDevice
import time


class EnhancedPositionController(Node):
    def __init__(self):

super().__init__('enhanced_position_controller')
        # Initialize PWM channels
        self.pwm_left = PWMOutputDevice(pin=18)
        self.pwm_right = PWMOutputDevice(pin=19)
        # Initialize encoders
        self.encoder_left =
DigitalInputDevice(pin=20)
        self.encoder_right =
DigitalInputDevice(pin=21)
        self.left_count = 0
        self.right_count = 0
        # Subscriber to position commands
        self.subscription =
self.create_subscription(
            Int32,
            'motor_position',
            self.position_callback,
            10)
        # Timer for feedback processing
```

```python
        self.timer = self.create_timer(0.05,
self.feedback_callback)
        self.target_position = 0
        self.get_logger().info('Enhanced Position
Controller Node Initialized.')

    def position_callback(self, msg):
        self.target_position = msg.data
        self.get_logger().info(f'Setting target
position to {self.target_position} steps.')
        self.move_to_position()

    def move_to_position(self):
        self.pwm_left.value = 0.5  # Set speed
(50%)
        self.pwm_right.value = 0.5
        self.get_logger().info('Motors started
moving towards target position.')

    def feedback_callback(self):
        # Read encoder states
        if self.encoder_left.value:
            self.left_count += 1
        if self.encoder_right.value:
            self.right_count += 1
        # Check if target position is reached
```

```python
        if self.left_count >=
self.target_position and self.right_count >=
self.target_position:
            self.stop()
        # Log encoder counts
        self.get_logger().info(f'Left Encoder:
{self.left_count}, Right Encoder:
{self.right_count}')

    def stop(self):
        self.pwm_left.value = 0.0
        self.pwm_right.value = 0.0
        self.get_logger().info('Reached target
position. Motors stopped.')

def main(args=None):
    rclpy.init(args=args)
    enhanced_position_controller =
EnhancedPositionController()
    rclpy.spin(enhanced_position_controller)
    enhanced_position_controller.destroy_node()
    rclpy.shutdown()

if __name__ == '__main__':
    main()
```

Explanation:

- **Enhanced Feedback Processing:** Checks encoder counts more frequently (every 0.05 seconds) for faster response.

- **Automatic Stopping:** Automatically stops motors when target position is reached based on encoder counts.

- **Logging:** Continuously logs encoder counts and state changes for monitoring.

Step 2: Update setup.py and Build the Package

```python
entry_points={
    'console_scripts': [
        'publisher =
my_robot_pkg.publisher:main',
        'subscriber =
my_robot_pkg.subscriber:main',
        'lidar_processor =
my_robot_pkg.lidar_processor:main',
        'camera_processor =
my_robot_pkg.camera_processor:main',
        'imu_processor =
my_robot_pkg.imu_processor:main',
        'motor_control =
my_robot_pkg.motor_control:main',
```

```
        'motor_control_feedback =
my_robot_pkg.motor_control_with_feedback:main',
        'speed_control =
my_robot_pkg.speed_control:main',
        'position_control =
my_robot_pkg.position_control:main',
        'enhanced_position_control =
my_robot_pkg.enhanced_position_control:main',
    ],
},
bash
```

```
cd ~/ros2_ws/
colcon build
source install/setup.bash
```

Step 3: Run the Enhanced Position Control Node

```
bash
```

```
ros2 run my_robot_pkg enhanced_position_control
```

Step 4: Send Position Commands

```
bash
```

```
ros2 topic pub /motor_position std_msgs/Int32
"data: 1500"
```

Expected Output:

```
less
```

```
[INFO] [enhanced_position_controller]: Setting
target position to 1500 steps.
[INFO] [enhanced_position_controller]: Motors
started moving towards target position.
[INFO] [enhanced_position_controller]: Left
Encoder: 1, Right Encoder: 1
...
[INFO] [enhanced_position_controller]: Reached
target position. Motors stopped.
```

Conclusion

Congratulations! You've successfully navigated through the intricacies of **Actuator Control and Motor Management,** mastering the art of controlling various actuators using ROS2 and Python. From understanding the fundamental types of actuators like DC motors, servos, and stepper motors to implementing advanced control techniques with PWM and motor drivers, you've built a solid foundation for creating responsive and precise robotic systems. Incorporating feedback mechanisms through encoders ensures that your robots can perform tasks with remarkable accuracy and reliability.

Key Takeaways:

1. **Diverse Actuator Types:** Each actuator type—DC motors, servos, and stepper motors—offers unique advantages suited to specific applications.

2. **ROS2 and Python Integration:** Leveraging ROS2's robust framework alongside Python's simplicity streamlines actuator control and system management.

3. **Precision Through Feedback:** Incorporating feedback mechanisms like encoders is essential for achieving precise motor control and responsive behavior.

4. **Hands-On Experience:** Engaging in hands-on projects solidifies theoretical knowledge, enhancing your ability to implement complex control systems.

Next Steps:

1. **Explore Advanced Control Algorithms:**

   o Implement PID (Proportional-Integral-Derivative) controllers for smoother and more accurate motor control.

   o Experiment with trajectory planning and dynamic motion adjustments based on sensor feedback.

2. **Integrate More Actuators:**

   o Add additional servos or stepper motors to expand your robot's capabilities.

   o Explore actuators like hydraulic or pneumatic systems for specialized applications.

3. **Enhance Feedback Systems:**

- o Incorporate more sophisticated sensors such as rotary encoders with higher resolution.

- o Utilize IMUs for comprehensive motion tracking and stability control.

4. **Develop Complex Projects:**

- o Build robotic arms with multiple degrees of freedom, controlled precisely using ROS2.

- o Create autonomous vehicles that navigate complex environments using integrated sensor and actuator systems.

Remember: *Mastery in robotics comes from continuous learning and experimentation. Don't hesitate to push the boundaries, experiment with new components, and seek out innovative solutions to challenges. With the skills acquired in this chapter, you're well-equipped to develop sophisticated, intelligent robots capable of performing complex tasks with precision and efficiency.*

Keep the momentum going—your journey in autonomous robotics is just beginning! Harness the power of actuators, refine your control strategies, and watch your robots come alive with movement and intelligence.

Summary

In Chapter 5, "Actuator Control and Motor Management," we delved into the essential role actuators play in enabling robotic movement and interaction. We explored the primary types of actuators—DC motors, servos, and stepper motors—understanding their unique characteristics and applications in various robotic systems. The chapter detailed how to control these actuators using ROS2 and Python, emphasizing the importance of PWM control and motor drivers for efficient and precise motor management.

We also examined the significance of feedback mechanisms, such as encoders, in achieving accurate and responsive actuator control. Through hands-on projects, you learned to implement speed and position control, integrating real-time feedback into ROS2 to enhance motor precision and reliability. These practical exercises reinforced theoretical concepts, providing a comprehensive understanding of how to manage and control actuators effectively within a ROS2 framework.

By mastering actuator control and motor management, you've equipped yourself with the skills necessary to develop responsive, precise, and intelligent robotic systems capable of performing complex tasks with high accuracy. This chapter serves as a crucial stepping stone towards more advanced robotics projects, laying the foundation for sophisticated motor control and dynamic robotic behaviors.

Chapter 6: Navigation and Mapping

Welcome to the fascinating realm of **Navigation and Mapping** in robotics! Picture your robot as an explorer venturing into the unknown. Just as a human relies on maps and navigational tools to traverse unfamiliar terrain, robots depend on sophisticated systems to understand and navigate their environments autonomously. This chapter will introduce you to **Simultaneous Localization and Mapping (SLAM)**, delve into key concepts and algorithms, explore popular SLAM solutions in ROS2, and guide you through path planning and obstacle avoidance. By the end, you'll undertake a hands-on project to build a navigational system, setting up **SLAM** with ROS2 and implementing autonomous navigation. Let's embark on this journey to empower your robot with the ability to see, understand, and move intelligently through its world!

Introduction to SLAM (Simultaneous Localization and Mapping)

Imagine walking through a dense forest with a friend. Neither of you has a map, but together, you create one as you explore, all while keeping track of your own position within the map. This collaborative creation and localization process is akin to **Simultaneous Localization and Mapping (SLAM)** in robotics.

What is SLAM?

SLAM is a computational problem where a robot must build a map of an unknown environment while simultaneously keeping track of its location within that map. It's a foundational technology enabling robots to navigate autonomously, whether in a cluttered warehouse, a sprawling outdoor area, or even inside your home.

Key Components of SLAM:

1. **Localization:** Determining the robot's position and orientation within the map.

2. **Mapping:** Building a representation of the robot's environment, typically as a 2D or 3D map.

Why is SLAM Important?

- **Autonomy:** Enables robots to operate without human intervention.

- **Adaptability:** Allows robots to navigate dynamic and previously unknown environments.

- **Efficiency:** Facilitates optimal path planning by understanding the environment.

How Does SLAM Work?

SLAM algorithms rely on data from various sensors (like LIDAR, cameras, and IMUs) to detect features in the environment. As the robot moves, it continuously updates its map and refines its position based on sensor feedback.

Analogy: Think of SLAM as drawing a map while navigating through a city. Each intersection you encounter adds detail to your map, and each step you take refines your understanding of your current location relative to the map.

SLAM Process Overview

```
+----------------------------------+
|          Robot Movement          |
+----------------------------------+
                 |
                 v
+----------------------------------+
|       Sensor Data Capture        |
|     (LIDAR, Camera, IMU)         |
+----------------------------------+
                 |
                 v
+----------------------------------+
|      Feature Extraction &        |
|        Data Association          |
+----------------------------------+
                 |
                 v
+----------------------------------+
|          Map Building            |
|       (2D/3D Environment)        |
+----------------------------------+
                 |
                 v
+----------------------------------+
|          Localization            |
|       (Robot's Position)         |
+----------------------------------+
                 |
                 v
+----------------------------------+
|       Continuous Refinement      |
|      (Loop Closure & Update)     |
+----------------------------------+
```

Diagram Explanation: This diagram outlines the SLAM process, highlighting the flow from robot movement and sensor data capture to feature extraction, map building, localization, and continuous refinement.

Key Concepts and Algorithms

Understanding the core concepts and algorithms underpinning SLAM is crucial for implementing effective navigation systems. Let's explore these foundational elements.

Core Concepts of SLAM

1. **Odometry:**

   - **Definition:** The use of data from motion sensors (like wheel encoders) to estimate the robot's change in position over time.

   - **Limitation:** Odometry accumulates errors over time, leading to drift.

2. **Loop Closure:**

   - **Definition:** Detecting when the robot returns to a previously visited location.

   - **Importance:** Corrects accumulated odometry errors, refining the map and localization.

3. **Data Association:**

- o **Definition:** Matching current sensor observations with existing map features.

- o **Purpose:** Ensures accurate localization and map consistency.

4. **Graph-Based SLAM:**

- o **Concept:** Representing the SLAM problem as a graph where nodes are robot poses and edges are constraints from sensor data.

- o **Advantage:** Facilitates optimization techniques to minimize errors across the entire map.

Popular SLAM Algorithms

1. **Extended Kalman Filter (EKF) SLAM:**

- o **Approach:** Uses probabilistic methods to estimate the robot's state and the map.

- o **Strength:** Effective for small to medium-sized environments.

- o **Limitation:** Computationally intensive as the map grows.

2. **Particle Filter SLAM (FastSLAM):**

- o **Approach:** Utilizes a set of particles to represent possible robot poses, each with its own map.

- o **Strength:** Scales better with larger environments.

- ○ **Limitation:** Can suffer from particle depletion in complex scenarios.

3. **Graph-Based SLAM (GTSAM):**

   - ○ **Approach:** Constructs a graph of poses and constraints, optimizing the entire structure for consistency.

   - ○ **Strength:** Highly accurate and efficient for large-scale mapping.

   - ○ **Limitation:** Requires robust data association to prevent incorrect loop closures.

4. **Graph-SLAM with Pose Graph Optimization:**

   - ○ **Approach:** Focuses on optimizing the graph structure representing the robot's trajectory and landmarks.

   - ○ **Strength:** Efficiently handles loop closures and large maps.

   - ○ **Limitation:** Relies heavily on accurate feature detection and matching.

Advanced SLAM Techniques

1. **Visual SLAM (vSLAM):**

   - ○ **Definition:** Uses visual data from cameras to perform SLAM.

   - ○ **Advantage:** Rich environmental information and low-cost sensors.

- o **Examples:** ORB-SLAM, LSD-SLAM.

2. **LIDAR-Based SLAM:**

   - o **Definition:** Utilizes LIDAR data for precise distance measurements and mapping.

   - o **Advantage:** High accuracy and robustness in various lighting conditions.

   - o **Examples:** GMapping, Hector SLAM.

3. **RGB-D SLAM:**

   - o **Definition:** Combines RGB (color) and Depth information from sensors like Kinect.

   - o **Advantage:** Provides both visual and depth data for enhanced mapping and localization.

   - o **Examples:** RTAB-Map, ElasticFusion.

Comparison of SLAM Algorithms

```
+--------------------+--------------------+--------------------+
|     Algorithm      |     Strengths      |    Limitations     |
+--------------------+--------------------+--------------------+
| EKF SLAM           | Accurate for small | Scales poorly with |
|                    | environments       | map size           |
+--------------------+--------------------+--------------------+
| Particle Filter    | Scales to larger   | Particle depletion |
| SLAM               | environments       | in complex scenarios |
+--------------------+--------------------+--------------------+
| Graph-Based SLAM   | High accuracy,     | Requires robust    |
|                    | efficient for large| data association   |
|                    | maps               |                    |
+--------------------+--------------------+--------------------+
| Visual SLAM        | Rich data from     | Sensitive to lighting |
|                    | cameras, low-cost  | conditions, feature |
|                    | sensors            | detection challenges |
+--------------------+--------------------+--------------------+
| LIDAR-Based SLAM   | High accuracy,     | Higher cost, heavy |
|                    | robust in lighting | data processing    |
+--------------------+--------------------+--------------------+
| RGB-D SLAM         | Combines visual and| Limited range, higher |
|                    | depth data         | power consumption  |
+--------------------+--------------------+--------------------+
```

Diagram Explanation: This table compares various SLAM algorithms, highlighting their strengths and limitations to help you choose the most suitable one for your application.

Popular SLAM Solutions in ROS2

ROS2 offers a plethora of SLAM solutions, each tailored to different applications and sensor configurations. Let's explore some of the most popular SLAM packages available in ROS2.

1. SLAM Toolbox

Overview: SLAM Toolbox is a versatile and efficient ROS2 package that provides real-time 2D SLAM capabilities. It supports both online and offline mapping, making it suitable for a wide range of applications.

Key Features:

- **Multi-Session Mapping:** Allows for the creation and merging of multiple maps.

- **Loop Closure Detection:** Automatically detects and corrects loop closures.

- **Map Persistence:** Saves and loads maps for reuse and sharing.

- **Flexible Configuration:** Easily adjustable parameters to suit different environments and sensor setups.

Installation:

```bash
```

```bash
sudo apt install ros-humble-slam-toolbox
```

Usage:

1. Launch SLAM Toolbox:

```bash
```

```bash
ros2 launch slam_toolbox online_async_launch.py
```

2. **Visualize in RViz:**

SLAM Toolbox integrates seamlessly with RViz for real-time map visualization and monitoring.

2. Cartographer

Overview: Developed by Google, Cartographer is a powerful SLAM library that supports both 2D and 3D mapping. It's known for its accuracy and efficiency, making it a favorite for complex robotic applications.

Key Features:

- **Real-Time SLAM:** Provides real-time mapping and localization.

- **Multi-Session SLAM:** Supports the management of multiple SLAM sessions.

- **3D Mapping:** Extends beyond 2D mapping to create detailed 3D maps.

- **Flexible Sensor Integration:** Compatible with various sensor types, including LIDAR and IMUs.

Installation:

```bash
sudo apt install ros-humble-cartographer ros-humble-cartographer-ros
```

Usage:

1. Configure Cartographer:

Customize Cartographer's configuration files to match your robot's sensor setup and environment.

2. Launch Cartographer:

```bash

ros2 launch cartographer_ros
cartographer.launch.py
```

3. Visualize in RViz:

Utilize RViz to monitor the mapping process and assess localization accuracy.

3. RTAB-Map (Real-Time Appearance-Based Mapping)

Overview: RTAB-Map is a versatile ROS2 package that offers both 2D and 3D SLAM capabilities. It excels in environments with dynamic objects and provides robust loop closure detection.

Key Features:

- **Visual SLAM:** Leverages camera data for SLAM, making it ideal for robots equipped with RGB-D cameras.

- **Dynamic Environment Handling:** Effectively manages dynamic objects without compromising map integrity.

- **Graph-Based SLAM:** Utilizes pose graph optimization for accurate map creation.

- **Extensive Visualization:** Offers comprehensive visualization tools within RViz.

Installation:

```bash
```

```bash
sudo apt install ros-humble-rtabmap-ros
```

Usage:

1. **Launch RTAB-Map:**

```bash
```

```bash
ros2 launch rtabmap_ros rtabmap.launch.py
```

2. **Visualize and Monitor:**

Use RViz to observe the mapping process, adjust parameters, and assess performance.

4. Hector SLAM

Overview: Hector SLAM is a high-performance 2D SLAM solution that doesn't rely on odometry data, making it suitable for aerial robots and other platforms where odometry is unreliable.

Key Features:

- **Odometry-Free SLAM:** Eliminates the need for odometry, relying solely on LIDAR data.

- **Real-Time Performance:** Offers fast and efficient mapping suitable for dynamic environments.

- **Easy Integration:** Simplifies sensor integration with minimal configuration.

- **Lightweight:** Optimized for platforms with limited computational resources.

Installation:

```bash
sudo apt install ros-humble-hector-slam
```

Usage:

1. **Launch Hector SLAM:**

```bash
ros2 launch hector_slam hector_slam_launch.py
```

2. **Monitor in RViz:**

Visualize the mapping process and adjust parameters as needed for optimal performance.

Choosing the Right SLAM Solution

Selecting the appropriate SLAM package depends on various factors, including the type of sensors you're using, the complexity of the environment, and the computational resources available. Here are some guidelines to help you choose:

- **Sensor Configuration:**

    - **LIDAR-Based:** SLAM Toolbox, Cartographer, Hector SLAM.

    - **Camera-Based:** RTAB-Map, Cartographer.

- **Environment Complexity:**

    - **Static Environments:** All SLAM packages perform well.

    - **Dynamic Environments:** RTAB-Map and Cartographer offer robust handling of dynamic objects.

- **Computational Resources:**

    - **High Resources:** Cartographer (especially 3D mapping).

    - **Limited Resources:** Hector SLAM, SLAM Toolbox.

SLAM Package Selection Guide

```
+----------------------------------+
|        SLAM Packages             |
+----------------------------------+
|                                  |
|   +--------------------------+   /
|   |   SLAM Toolbox           |   |
|   |   - LIDAR-based          |   |
|   |   - 2D/3D Mapping        |   |
|   |   - Real-Time            |   |
|   +--------------------------+   /
|                                  |
|   +--------------------------+   /
|   |     Cartographer         |   |
|   |   - LIDAR & Camera       |   |
|   |   - 2D/3D Mapping        |   |
|   |   - High Accuracy        |   |
|   +--------------------------+   /
|                                  |
|   +--------------------------+   /
|   |      RTAB-Map            |   |
|   |   - Visual SLAM          |   |
|   |   - Dynamic Handling     |   |
|   |   - 2D/3D Mapping        |   |
|   +--------------------------+   /


|                             |
|   +----------------------+   /
|   |     Hector SLAM      |   |
|   |   - Odometry-Free    |   |
|   |   - High Performance |   |
|   |   - 2D Mapping       |   |
|   +----------------------+   /
|                             |
+-----------------------------+
```

Diagram Explanation: This guide helps you match your robot's sensor configuration and environmental requirements with the most suitable SLAM package.

Path Planning and Obstacle Avoidance

Once your robot can map its environment and understand its location, the next step is to enable it to move intelligently within that map. **Path Planning** and **Obstacle Avoidance** are critical components that ensure your robot can navigate from point A to point B efficiently and safely.

Path Planning

Path Planning involves determining an optimal route for the robot to reach its destination while avoiding obstacles. It's akin to finding the best route on a map, considering traffic, roadblocks, and other variables.

Key Objectives:

- **Optimality:** Find the shortest or fastest path.

- **Efficiency:** Minimize computational resources and time.

- **Robustness:** Adapt to dynamic changes in the environment.

Popular Path Planning Algorithms:

1. *A (A-Star):**
   - ○ **Approach:** Uses heuristics to find the least-cost path.

- o **Strength:** Guarantees the shortest path with an admissible heuristic.

- o **Limitation:** Can be computationally intensive for large maps.

2. **Dijkstra's Algorithm:**

- o **Approach:** Explores all possible paths systematically.

- o **Strength:** Guarantees the shortest path.

- o **Limitation:** Slower than A^* due to lack of heuristics.

3. **Rapidly-exploring Random Trees (RRT):**

- o **Approach:** Grows a tree of possible paths randomly, focusing on unexplored areas.

- o **Strength:** Efficient for high-dimensional spaces.

- o **Limitation:** May not find the optimal path.

4. **Probabilistic Roadmaps (PRM):**

- o **Approach:** Creates a roadmap of random nodes connected by feasible paths.

- o **Strength:** Suitable for multi-query environments.

- o **Limitation:** Requires extensive preprocessing.

5. **Potential Fields:**

- o **Approach:** Treats the robot as a point under the influence of attractive and repulsive fields.

- o **Strength:** Simple and intuitive.

- o **Limitation:** Can get stuck in local minima.

Obstacle Avoidance

Obstacle Avoidance ensures that the robot can dynamically adjust its path in real-time to prevent collisions with unexpected obstacles. It's like driving a car and steering around pedestrians or debris that suddenly appear.

Key Strategies:

1. **Reactive Methods:**

    - o **Description:** Make immediate adjustments based on sensor data without planning.

    - o **Examples:** Vector Field Histogram, Dynamic Window Approach.

2. **Predictive Methods:**

    - o **Description:** Anticipate obstacles and plan paths accordingly.

    - o **Examples:** Model Predictive Control, Velocity Obstacles.

3. **Hybrid Methods:**

    - o **Description:** Combine reactive and predictive approaches for robust performance.

    - o **Examples:** Combining A^* with Dynamic Window Approach.

Popular Obstacle Avoidance Algorithms:

1. **Dynamic Window Approach (DWA):**

   o **Approach:** Considers the robot's dynamic constraints to evaluate possible velocities.

   o **Strength:** Balances between exploration and safety.

   o **Limitation:** Computationally intensive for complex scenarios.

2. **Vector Field Histogram (VFH):**

   o **Approach:** Creates a histogram grid around the robot to identify safe directions.

   o **Strength:** Efficient and effective for real-time obstacle avoidance.

   o **Limitation:** Limited in handling highly dynamic environments.

3. **Elastic Bands:**

   o **Approach:** Represents the path as a flexible band that can stretch and bend around obstacles.

   o **Strength:** Smooth and adaptable to changing environments.

   o **Limitation:** Requires continuous sensor data for dynamic adjustments.

Integration with ROS2 Navigation Stack

ROS2 offers a comprehensive **Navigation Stack** that integrates SLAM, path planning, and obstacle avoidance, providing a seamless solution for autonomous navigation.

Key Components:

1. **Move Base:** Central node that manages path planning and obstacle avoidance.

2. **Costmap:** Represents the environment, marking obstacles and free space.

3. **Planner Plugins:** Implement various path planning algorithms.

4. **Controller Plugins:** Handle the execution of planned paths.

Popular Navigation Packages in ROS2:

- **Nav2 (Navigation 2):** The successor to the ROS1 Navigation Stack, providing enhanced capabilities and modularity.

ROS2 Navigation Stack Architecture

```
+--------------------------------+
|        Navigation Stack        |
+--------------------------------+
|                                |
|   +------------------------+   /
|   |      Move Base         |   |
|   +-----------+------------+   /
|               |                |
|   +-----------+------------+   /
|   |        Planner         |   |
|   +-----------+------------+   /
|               |                |
|   +-----------+------------+   /
|   |       Controller       |   |
|   +-----------+------------+   /
|               |                |
|   +-----------+------------+   /
|   |        Costmap         |   |
|   +-----------+------------+   /
|               |                |
|   +-----------+------------+   /
|   |      Sensor Data       |   |
|   +------------------------+   /
|                                |
+--------------------------------+
```

Diagram Explanation: This architecture diagram showcases the components of the **ROS2** Navigation Stack, illustrating how sensor data feeds into the costmap, which informs the planner and controller to execute navigation commands.

Real-Time Obstacle Detection and Avoidance

Even with a well-planned path, the dynamic nature of real-world environments necessitates real-time obstacle detection and avoidance. Your robot must be able to respond swiftly to unexpected obstacles to maintain safety and efficiency.

Strategies for Real-Time Obstacle Avoidance:

1. **Reactive Control:**

   - **Description:** Adjusts the robot's path on-the-fly based on immediate sensor inputs.

   - **Example:** Steering away when an obstacle is detected directly ahead.

2. **Behavior-Based Control:**

   - **Description:** Implements predefined behaviors (e.g., follow wall, avoid obstacle) that dictate the robot's actions.

   - **Example:** Switching between behaviors based on sensor data to navigate complex environments.

3. **Dynamic Path Replanning:**

   - **Description:** Continuously updates the planned path as new obstacles are detected.

o **Example:** Recalculating the route when a new obstacle blocks the current path.

Implementing Real-Time Obstacle Avoidance in ROS2:

Using the Dynamic Window Approach (DWA):

DWA is a popular method for obstacle avoidance that evaluates feasible velocities within dynamic constraints to select the best command.

1. **Configure DWA Parameters:**

   o **Velocity Constraints:** Define maximum and minimum speeds.

   o **Acceleration Constraints:** Set limits on how quickly the robot can accelerate or decelerate.

   o **Obstacle Distance:** Specify the minimum safe distance from obstacles.

2. **Integrate with Nav2:**

   o Nav2's planner can incorporate DWA for dynamic obstacle avoidance by configuring the appropriate controller plugin.

3. **Tune Parameters:**

   o Adjust parameters based on your robot's capabilities and the environment's complexity to achieve optimal performance.

Example: Configuring DWA in Nav2

yaml

```yaml
controller_server:
  ros__parameters:
    use_sim_time: false
    controller_frequency: 20.0
    min_vel_x: 0.0
    max_vel_x: 1.0
    min_vel_y: 0.0
    max_vel_y: 0.0
    min_vel_theta: -1.0
    max_vel_theta: 1.0
    acc_lim_x: 2.5
    acc_lim_y: 0.0
    acc_lim_theta: 3.2
    xy_goal_tolerance: 0.2
    yaw_goal_tolerance: 0.1
    dwa:
      use_dwa: true
      # Additional DWA-specific parameters
```

Explanation: This YAML configuration snippet sets up the DWA parameters within Nav2's controller server, defining velocity and acceleration limits, as well as goal tolerances.

Hands-On Project: Building a Navigational System

Ready to apply what you've learned? Let's embark on a hands-on project to build a complete navigational system for your robot, integrating SLAM, path planning, and obstacle avoidance using ROS2. This project will empower your robot to autonomously navigate through its environment with precision and reliability.

Setting Up SLAM with ROS2

Objective: Configure and launch a SLAM system using ROS2 to enable your robot to map its environment and localize itself within that map.

Components Needed:

1. **Robot Platform:** Equipped with LIDAR, camera, and IMU sensors.

2. **ROS2 Installation:** Ensure ROS2 (preferably Humble Hawksbill) is installed and configured.

3. **SLAM Package:** Choose a suitable SLAM package (e.g., SLAM Toolbox, Cartographer).

4. **Computational Resources:** Adequate processing power (e.g., Raspberry Pi 4, NVIDIA Jetson).

Step-by-Step Setup:

Step 1: Install and Configure SLAM Package

Example Using SLAM Toolbox:

1. **Install SLAM Toolbox:**

```bash
bash
```

```bash
sudo apt install ros-humble-slam-toolbox
```

2. **Create a Launch File:**

Create a new launch file within your ROS2 package to initialize SLAM Toolbox.

```python
python
```

```python
# slam_toolbox_launch.py
from launch import LaunchDescription
from launch_ros.actions import Node

def generate_launch_description():
    return LaunchDescription([
        Node(
            package='slam_toolbox',
            executable='sync_slam_toolbox_node',
            name='slam_toolbox',
            output='screen',
            parameters=[{'use_sim_time': False}]
        )
    ])
```

3. Launch SLAM Toolbox:

```bash
```

```
ros2 launch my_robot_pkg slam_toolbox_launch.py
```

Step 2: Visualize the Map in RViz

1. Launch RViz:

```bash
```

```
rviz2
```

2. Configure RViz:

- o **Add Map Display:** Subscribe to the /map topic to visualize the generated map.

- o **Add Robot Model:** Display the robot's current pose.

- o **Add LaserScan:** Visualize LIDAR data.

3. Start Robot Movement:

- o Begin moving your robot to allow SLAM Toolbox to start mapping and localization.

Implementing Autonomous Navigation

With SLAM in place, the next step is to enable your robot to navigate autonomously from one location to another within its mapped environment.

Step-by-Step Implementation:

Step 1: Install and Configure Nav2

1. **Install Nav2 Packages:**

bash

```
sudo apt install ros-humble-nav2-bringup
```

2. **Create a Navigation Launch File:**

python

```
# navigation_launch.py
from launch import LaunchDescription
from launch_ros.actions import Node

def generate_launch_description():
    return LaunchDescription([
        Node(
            package='nav2_bringup',
            executable='bringup_launch.py',
            name='nav2_bringup',
            output='screen',
            parameters=[
                {'use_sim_time': False},
                {'autostart': True},
                # Add additional parameters as
needed
            ]
        )
```

```
])
```

3. Launch Nav2:

```bash
ros2 launch my_robot_pkg navigation_launch.py
```

Step 2: Configure Costmaps

1. Define Global and Local Costmaps:

- **Global Costmap:** Represents the entire environment, used for long-term planning.

- **Local Costmap:** Focuses on the immediate vicinity, used for short-term planning and obstacle avoidance.

2. Adjust Parameters:

- Set resolution, size, inflation radius, and sensor sources based on your environment and robot's capabilities.

Step 3: Configure Path Planner and Controller

1. Select Planner Plugin:

- **Example:** NavfnPlanner for A* algorithm.

2. Select Controller Plugin:

- **Example:** DWAPlanner for Dynamic Window Approach.

3. Adjust Planner and Controller Parameters:

- o Optimize for speed, safety, and efficiency based on your robot's requirements.

Nav2 Configuration Overview

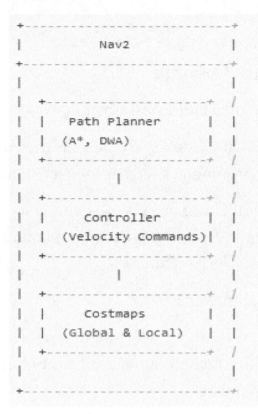

Diagram Explanation: This overview shows how Nav2 integrates the path planner and controller with the costmaps to execute autonomous navigation commands.

Testing Autonomous Navigation

1. **Set a Navigation Goal:**

Use RViz or command-line tools to send a navigation goal to your robot.

bash

```
ros2 action send_goal /navigate_to_pose
nav2_msgs/action/NavigateToPose "{pose:
{position: {x: 2.0, y: 3.0}, orientation: {w:
1.0}}}"
```

2. **Monitor in RViz:**

   o Observe the planned path and the robot's movement towards the goal.

   o Watch for real-time updates in the costmaps and obstacle avoidance maneuvers.

3. **Adjust Parameters as Needed:**

   o Fine-tune planner and controller parameters to optimize navigation performance.

Autonomous Navigation Flowchart

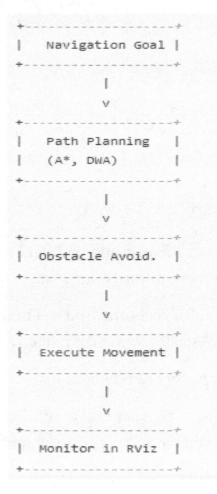

Diagram Explanation: This flowchart outlines the steps from receiving a navigation goal to planning a path, avoiding obstacles, executing movement commands, and monitoring the process in RViz.

Conclusion

Congratulations! You've successfully navigated through the complexities of **Navigation and Mapping,** equipping your robot with the ability to autonomously traverse its environment with precision and intelligence. By understanding and implementing SLAM, path planning, and obstacle avoidance, you've laid a robust foundation for advanced robotic functionalities.

Key Takeaways:

1. **SLAM Mastery:** Grasped the essentials of Simultaneous Localization and Mapping, enabling your robot to understand and map its environment while tracking its position.

2. **Path Planning Proficiency:** Explored various path planning algorithms, understanding their strengths and limitations to choose the most suitable one for your application.

3. **Obstacle Avoidance Skills:** Learned strategies for real-time obstacle detection and avoidance, ensuring your robot can navigate safely in dynamic environments.

4. **ROS2 Integration:** Leveraged ROS2's powerful Navigation Stack to seamlessly integrate SLAM, path planning, and obstacle avoidance into a cohesive system.

5. **Hands-On Experience:** Built and configured a navigational system, gaining practical insights into the deployment and tuning of autonomous navigation components.

Next Steps:

1. **Enhance SLAM and Navigation:**

   o Experiment with 3D SLAM for more complex environments.

   o Integrate additional sensors like GPS for outdoor navigation.

2. **Advanced Path Planning:**

   o Implement multi-robot path planning for collaborative tasks.

   o Explore dynamic replanning in highly unpredictable environments.

3. **Incorporate Machine Learning:**

   o Utilize machine learning techniques to improve obstacle detection and decision-making.

   o Implement predictive models for anticipating environmental changes.

4. **Deploy in Real-World Scenarios:**

   o Test your navigational system in diverse settings, from warehouses to outdoor terrains.

   o Optimize performance based on field observations and feedback.

Remember: *Autonomous navigation is a multifaceted domain that combines perception, planning, and control. Continuous experimentation, learning, and adaptation are* *key to mastering these skills and pushing the boundaries of what your robot can achieve.*

You're now well-equipped to build intelligent, autonomous robots capable of navigating and mapping their environments with finesse! Embrace the challenges, explore new possibilities, and continue your journey towards creating sophisticated robotic systems.

Summary

In Chapter 6, "Navigation and Mapping," we delved into the pivotal role of **Simultaneous Localization and Mapping (SLAM)** in enabling robots to autonomously navigate their environments. We explored the fundamental concepts and algorithms that underpin SLAM, including odometry, loop closure, and various SLAM algorithms like EKF, Particle Filter, and Graph-Based SLAM. The chapter highlighted popular SLAM solutions in ROS2, such as SLAM Toolbox, Cartographer, RTAB-Map, and Hector SLAM, providing insights into their features and appropriate use cases.

We then transitioned to **Path Planning and Obstacle Avoidance**, examining efficient algorithms like A*, Dijkstra's, RRT, PRM, and Dynamic Window Approach (DWA). Understanding these algorithms is crucial for enabling robots to determine optimal paths and navigate safely in dynamic environments. The integration of real-time obstacle avoidance strategies ensures that robots can adapt to unexpected changes and maintain safety.

Through a comprehensive hands-on project, you set up a SLAM system using ROS2, configured the Navigation Stack, and implemented autonomous navigation capabilities. This practical experience reinforced theoretical knowledge, demonstrating how to configure SLAM packages, set up costmaps, select appropriate planners and controllers, and execute navigation commands effectively.

By mastering Navigation and Mapping, you've equipped your robot with the essential tools to perceive, understand, and move intelligently within its environment. This chapter serves as a critical milestone in your robotics journey, paving the way for more advanced applications and sophisticated autonomous behaviors.

Chapter 7: Behavior Control and State Machines

Welcome to the dynamic sphere of **Behavior Control and State Machines** in robotics! Imagine your robot as a skilled conductor orchestrating a symphony—each behavior is a musical note, and the state machine ensures harmonious execution. Just as a conductor directs musicians to create a cohesive performance, behavior control systems guide robots to perform complex tasks seamlessly. This chapter demystifies the concepts of Behavior Trees and State Machines, explores their differences and applications, and provides hands-on experience in implementing intelligent behaviors using ROS2 and Python. By the end, you'll be adept at designing and integrating sophisticated behavior control systems, empowering your robots with autonomy and adaptability.

Understanding Behavior Trees and State Machines

Robotic systems thrive on structured decision-making processes that dictate how they respond to varying situations. **Behavior Trees** and **State Machines** are two foundational approaches to managing these decisions. While they share similarities in controlling robot behavior, their structures and applications differ significantly.

Concepts and Differences

State Machines

State Machines, particularly Finite State Machines (FSMs), are a traditional method for modeling behavior in systems where the robot can be in one of a finite number of states at any given time. Transitions between these states are triggered by events or conditions.

Key Components:

1. **States:** Distinct modes or conditions (e.g., Idle, Moving, Charging).

2. **Transitions:** Rules that define how the system moves from one state to another based on events or conditions.

3. **Events/Conditions:** Triggers that cause state transitions (e.g., battery low, obstacle detected).

Example:

Consider a robot vacuum cleaner with the following states:

- **Idle:** The robot is stationary and waiting for commands.

- **Cleaning:** The robot is actively vacuuming.

- **Returning to Dock:** The robot is navigating back to its charging station.

- **Charging:** The robot is recharging its battery.

Transitions occur based on conditions like battery level or user commands.

Advantages:

- **Simplicity:** Easy to design and understand for straightforward behaviors.

- **Predictability:** Clear paths and transitions make debugging easier.

Limitations:

- **Scalability:** Becomes complex and unwieldy as the number of states increases.

- **Flexibility:** Rigid structure can make it difficult to handle dynamic and unexpected scenarios.

Behavior Trees

Behavior Trees (BTs) are a more recent approach that offers greater flexibility and scalability compared to State Machines. Originally developed in the gaming industry, BTs have gained popularity in robotics for managing complex behaviors.

Key Components:

1. **Nodes:** Building blocks representing actions, conditions, or control flow elements.

2. **Control Flow Nodes:** Define the execution order and decision-making logic (e.g., Sequence, Selector).

3. **Leaf Nodes:** Perform actions or evaluate conditions.

Behavior Tree Types:

- **Sequence:** Executes child nodes in order until one fails.

- **Selector:** Executes child nodes in order until one succeeds.

- **Parallel:** Executes multiple child nodes simultaneously.

Example:

A robot assisting a user might have the following behavior tree structure:

- **Root Selector:**
  - **Sequence:**
    - Check if user needs assistance.
    - Approach user.
    - Provide assistance.
  - **Sequence:**
    - Monitor battery level.
    - If low, navigate to charging station.

Advantages:

- **Modularity:** Easily reusable and composable behaviors.

- **Scalability:** Handles complex behaviors without exponential state growth.

- **Flexibility:** More adaptable to dynamic and unpredictable environments.

Limitations:

- **Complexity:** Initial design can be more complex compared to simple State Machines.

- **Learning Curve:** Requires understanding of tree-based logic structures.

When to Use Each Approach

Choosing between State Machines and Behavior Trees depends on the complexity and requirements of your robotic application.

Use State Machines When:

- The robot's behavior is relatively simple and linear.

- There are a limited number of states and transitions.

- Predictable and easily manageable behaviors are sufficient.

Use Behavior Trees When:

- The robot needs to perform complex, hierarchical behaviors.

- Reusability and modularity of behaviors are important.

- The environment is dynamic, requiring adaptable and flexible decision-making.

- Scalability is a concern, especially in larger projects.

Analogy:

- **State Machines** are like a traffic light system, with fixed states (red, yellow, green) and predictable transitions.

- **Behavior Trees** are like a skilled chef preparing a complex meal, adjusting recipes and techniques based on real-time feedback and ingredient availability.

State Machine vs. Behavior Tree Comparison

```
+---------------------+        +-----------------------------+
|    State Machine    |        |        Behavior Tree        |
+---------------------+        +-----------------------------+
|                     |        |                             |
|   +----------+      |        |  +-----------+              |
|   | State    |      |        |  | Selector|                |
|   | Idle     |------|--------|-->+---------+----+          |
|   +----------+      |        |  | Sequence |   |           |
|        |            |        |  +----------+   |           |
|        v            |        |       |         |           |
|   +----------+      |        |       v         |           |
|   | Cleaning|       |        |  +----------+    |           |
|   +----------+      |        |  | Approach|     |           |
|        |            |        |  +----------+    |           |
|        v            |        |       |          |           |
|   +----------+      |        |  +----------+     |          |
|   | Returning|      |        |  |Provide  |      |          |
|   +----------+      |        |  |Assistance|     |          |
|                     |        |  +----------+     |          |
+---------------------+        +-----------------------------+
```

Diagram Explanation: This diagram contrasts a simple State Machine with a Behavior Tree, illustrating how BTs offer hierarchical and modular control structures compared to the linear and rigid nature of FSMs.

Implementing Behavior Control in ROS2

ROS2 (Robot Operating System 2) provides a robust framework for implementing behavior control systems, whether using State Machines or Behavior Trees. This section will guide you through the tools and libraries available in ROS2 for behavior control, focusing on Behavior Trees and State Machines, and demonstrate how to manage state and behavior using Python.

ROS2 Behavior Tree Libraries

Behavior Trees have gained traction in ROS2 due to their flexibility and scalability. Several libraries facilitate the creation and integration of BTs within ROS2 environments.

1. py_trees

Overview:

py_trees is a popular Python library for creating Behavior Trees. It offers an intuitive API and integrates seamlessly with ROS2, making it a go-to choice for developers.

Key Features:

- **Hierarchical Structure:** Easily define complex behaviors through tree-like structures.

- **Modular Nodes:** Reusable nodes for actions, conditions, and control flow.

- **Visualization:** Tools for visualizing the Behavior Tree structure and execution flow.

- **Logging and Debugging:** Built-in support for logging node statuses and debugging.

Installation:

```bash
```

```bash
pip3 install py_trees
```

Example Usage:

```python
```

```python
import py_trees

def create_behavior_tree():
    root = py_trees.composites.Selector("Root")

    # First sequence: Check if battery is low
    battery_sequence =
py_trees.composites.Sequence("Battery Check")
    check_battery = CheckBattery()
    navigate_to_charge = NavigateToCharge()
```

```
    battery_sequence.add_children([check_battery,
navigate_to_charge])


    # Second sequence: Perform cleaning
    cleaning_sequence =
py_trees.composites.Sequence("Cleaning")
    start_cleaning = StartCleaning()
    perform_cleaning = PerformCleaning()


cleaning_sequence.add_children([start_cleaning,
perform_cleaning])


    # Add sequences to root
    root.add_children([battery_sequence,
cleaning_sequence])


    return root
```

2. BehaviorTree.CPP

Overview:

BehaviorTree.CPP is a C++ library for Behavior Trees, offering high performance and integration with ROS2. It's suitable for applications where speed and efficiency are critical.

Key Features:

- **Real-Time Execution:** Optimized for real-time systems.

- **ROS2 Integration:** Built-in support for ROS2 nodes and communication.

- **Extensibility:** Easily extendable with custom nodes and plugins.

- **Thread Safety:** Designed for concurrent executions and multi-threaded environments.

Installation:

```bash

sudo apt install ros-humble-behaviortree-cpp-v3
```

Example Usage:

```cpp

#include "behaviortree_cpp_v3/bt_factory.h"

int main(int argc, char **argv)
{
    BT::BehaviorTreeFactory factory;

    factory.registerSimpleAction("SayHello",
[](){
        std::cout << "Hello, Behavior Tree!" <<
std::endl;
        return BT::NodeStatus::SUCCESS;
    });
```

```
auto tree = factory.createTreeFromText(R"(
    <root main_tree_to_execute="MainTree">
        <BehaviorTree ID="MainTree">
            <SayHello/>
        </BehaviorTree>
    </root>
)");
tree.tickRoot();
return 0;
}
```

State Management with Python

Managing states in ROS2 using Python can be achieved through various approaches, including custom implementations or leveraging existing libraries like smach or flexbe. However, Behavior Trees offer a more scalable and flexible solution for complex behaviors.

1. State Machines with smach

While smach is more prominent in ROS1, it's still usable in ROS2 with some adjustments. However, for a more ROS2-native approach, Behavior Trees are recommended.

2. State Management with py_trees

py_trees inherently manages state through its Behavior Trees, eliminating the need for separate state machine frameworks. Each node in a BT represents a behavior with its own state, seamlessly integrated into the tree structure.

Example: Simple Behavior Tree with py_trees

```python
import py_trees
import rclpy
from rclpy.node import Node

class CheckBattery(py_trees.behaviour.Behaviour):
    def __init__(self, name="Check Battery"):
        super(CheckBattery, self).__init__(name)
        self.battery_low = False

    def update(self):
        # Simulate battery check
        if self.battery_low:
            return py_trees.common.Status.SUCCESS
        else:
            return py_trees.common.Status.FAILURE

class NavigateToCharge(py_trees.behaviour.Behaviour):
    def __init__(self, name="Navigate to Charge"):
        super(NavigateToCharge, self).__init__(name)

    def update(self):
```

```python
        print("Navigating to charging
station...")
        return py_trees.common.Status.SUCCESS


class
StartCleaning(py_trees.behaviour.Behaviour):
    def __init__(self, name="Start Cleaning"):
        super(StartCleaning, self).__init__(name)

    def update(self):
        print("Starting cleaning...")
        return py_trees.common.Status.SUCCESS


class
PerformCleaning(py_trees.behaviour.Behaviour):
    def __init__(self, name="Perform Cleaning"):
        super(PerformCleaning,
self).__init__(name)

    def update(self):
        print("Performing cleaning...")
        return py_trees.common.Status.SUCCESS


def main(args=None):
    rclpy.init(args=args)
    node = Node("behavior_tree_node")

    root = create_behavior_tree()
```

```python
    behaviour_tree =
py_trees.trees.BehaviourTree(root)

    try:
        while rclpy.ok():
            behaviour_tree.tick()
            rclpy.spin_once(node,
timeout_sec=0.1)
    except KeyboardInterrupt:
        pass

    node.destroy_node()
    rclpy.shutdown()

def create_behavior_tree():
    root = py_trees.composites.Selector("Root")

    # Battery check sequence
    battery_sequence =
py_trees.composites.Sequence("Battery Check")
    check_battery = CheckBattery()
    navigate_to_charge = NavigateToCharge()
    battery_sequence.add_children([check_battery,
navigate_to_charge])

    # Cleaning sequence
    cleaning_sequence =
py_trees.composites.Sequence("Cleaning")
```

```
    start_cleaning = StartCleaning()
    perform_cleaning = PerformCleaning()

cleaning_sequence.add_children([start_cleaning,
perform_cleaning])

    # Add sequences to root
    root.add_children([battery_sequence,
cleaning_sequence])

    return root


if __name__ == "__main__":
    main()
```

Explanation:

- **Behavior Nodes:** Each behavior node (CheckBattery, NavigateToCharge, etc.) encapsulates a specific task with its own state and logic.

- **Selector:** The root node that prioritizes sequences; if the first sequence fails, it proceeds to the next.

- **Sequence:** Groups related behaviors; all must succeed for the sequence to succeed.

- **Main Loop:** Continuously ticks the behavior tree, allowing dynamic behavior execution based on conditions.

py_trees Behavior Tree Structure

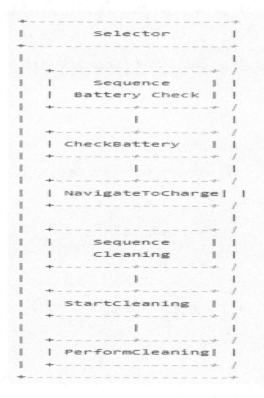

Diagram Explanation: This diagram illustrates a simple Behavior Tree structure created with py_trees, showcasing how sequences are organized under a selector to manage behaviors based on conditions.

Hands-On Project: Creating Intelligent Behaviors

Building intelligent behaviors transforms your robot from a reactive machine into an autonomous agent capable of complex task execution. In this hands-on project, you'll design a Behavior Tree for task execution and integrate it with ROS2 nodes, leveraging the power of py_trees to orchestrate your robot's actions intelligently.

Designing a Behavior Tree for Task Execution

Objective: Create a Behavior Tree that allows the robot to perform cleaning tasks, monitor its battery level, and navigate to the charging station when necessary.

Components Needed:

1. **Robot Platform:** Equipped with actuators (motors), sensors (battery monitor, LIDAR), and a ROS2 setup.

2. **ROS2 Packages:** py_trees, rclpy, and necessary sensor drivers.

3. **Python Environment:** For scripting Behavior Tree nodes.

Step-by-Step Design:

Step 1: Define the Robot's Behaviors

Identify the primary behaviors your robot needs to perform. For this project:

1. **Check Battery Level:** Continuously monitor the battery to determine if charging is needed.

2. **Navigate to Charging Station:** Move towards the charging dock when the battery is low.

3. **Start Cleaning:** Begin the cleaning process when the battery is sufficient.

4. **Perform Cleaning:** Execute the cleaning task.

5. **Return to Idle:** Stop actions and remain idle when tasks are complete or charging is in progress.

Step 2: Create Custom Behavior Nodes

Implement custom nodes for each behavior using py_trees.

Example: NavigateToCharge Node

python

```python
import py_trees
import rclpy
from rclpy.node import Node
from geometry_msgs.msg import Twist


class
NavigateToCharge(py_trees.behaviour.Behaviour):
    def __init__(self, name="Navigate To Charge",
ros_node=None):
        super(NavigateToCharge,
self).__init__(name)
        self.ros_node = ros_node
        self.publisher =
self.ros_node.create_publisher(Twist, 'cmd_vel',
10)
        self.move_cmd = Twist()
```

```python
        self.move_cmd.linear.x = 0.3   # Move
forward at 0.3 m/s
        self.move_cmd.angular.z = 0.0
        self.goal_reached = False


    def update(self):
        if not self.goal_reached:
            self.publisher.publish(self.move_cmd)

self.ros_node.get_logger().info("Navigating to
charging station...")
            # Simulate goal reached after some
time
            # In a real scenario, use sensor
feedback to determine when to stop
            self.goal_reached = True
            return py_trees.common.Status.RUNNING
        else:
            self.move_cmd.linear.x = 0.0
            self.move_cmd.angular.z = 0.0
            self.publisher.publish(self.move_cmd)

self.ros_node.get_logger().info("Reached charging
station.")
            return py_trees.common.Status.SUCCESS
```

Explanation:

- **NavigateToCharge Node:** Commands the robot to move towards the charging station.

- **Simulated Goal Reached:** In a real implementation, sensor data (like LIDAR or GPS) would determine when the robot arrives.

Step 3: Assemble the Behavior Tree

Combine all custom nodes into a cohesive Behavior Tree structure.

Example: Behavior Tree Assembly

```python

import py_trees
import rclpy
from rclpy.node import Node

def create_behavior_tree(ros_node):
    root = py_trees.composites.Selector("Root")

    # Battery check sequence
    battery_sequence =
py_trees.composites.Sequence("Battery Check")
    battery_monitor =
BatteryMonitor(ros_node=ros_node)
    navigate_to_charge =
NavigateToCharge(ros_node=ros_node)

battery_sequence.add_children([battery_monitor,
navigate_to_charge])
```

```python
    # Cleaning sequence
    cleaning_sequence =
py_trees.composites.Sequence("Cleaning")
    start_cleaning =
StartCleaning(ros_node=ros_node)
    perform_cleaning =
PerformCleaning(ros_node=ros_node)

cleaning_sequence.add_children([start_cleaning,
perform_cleaning])

    # Add sequences to root
    root.add_children([battery_sequence,
cleaning_sequence])

    return root

class
BatteryMonitor(py_trees.behaviour.Behaviour):
    def __init__(self, name="Battery Monitor",
ros_node=None):
        super(BatteryMonitor,
self).__init__(name)
        self.ros_node = ros_node
        self.battery_level = 100.0
        self.subscription =
self.ros_node.create_subscription(
            Float32,
```

```
            'battery_level',
            self.battery_callback,
            10)
        self.subscription  # prevent unused
variable warning

    def battery_callback(self, msg):
        self.battery_level = msg.data
        self.logger.info(f'Battery level updated:
{self.battery_level}%')


    def update(self):
        if self.battery_level < 20.0:
            return py_trees.common.Status.SUCCESS
        else:
            return py_trees.common.Status.FAILURE

class
StartCleaning(py_trees.behaviour.Behaviour):
    def __init__(self, name="Start Cleaning",
ros_node=None):
        super(StartCleaning, self).__init__(name)
        self.ros_node = ros_node
        self.publisher =
self.ros_node.create_publisher(String, 'cmd_vel',
10)
        self.move_cmd = Twist()
```

```python
        self.move_cmd.linear.x = 0.2   # Move
forward at 0.2 m/s
        self.move_cmd.angular.z = 0.0
        self.started = False


    def update(self):
        if not self.started:
            self.publisher.publish(self.move_cmd)

self.ros_node.get_logger().info("Starting
cleaning...")
            self.started = True
            return py_trees.common.Status.RUNNING
        else:
            # Simulate cleaning completion
            self.started = False
            return py_trees.common.Status.SUCCESS

class
PerformCleaning(py_trees.behaviour.Behaviour):
    def __init__(self, name="Perform Cleaning",
ros_node=None):
        super(PerformCleaning,
self).__init__(name)
        self.ros_node = ros_node
        self.publisher =
self.ros_node.create_publisher(String, 'cmd_vel',
10)
```

```
        self.move_cmd = Twist()
        self.move_cmd.linear.x = 0.0   # Stop
movement
        self.move_cmd.angular.z = 0.0
        self.cleaned = False


    def update(self):
        if not self.cleaned:
            self.publisher.publish(self.move_cmd)


self.ros_node.get_logger().info("Cleaning in
progress...")
            # Simulate cleaning time
            time.sleep(2)
            self.cleaned = True
            return py_trees.common.Status.SUCCESS
        else:
            return py_trees.common.Status.SUCCESS
```

Explanation:

- **BatteryMonitor:** Monitors battery level and triggers navigation to the charging station if low.

- **StartCleaning and PerformCleaning:** Manage the cleaning process, simulating start and completion of tasks.

- **Root Selector:** Prioritizes battery check; if the battery is low, it navigates to charge; otherwise, it proceeds to clean.

Step 4: Integrate with ROS2 Nodes

Ensure that the Behavior Tree runs within a ROS2 node, allowing seamless communication with other system components.

Example: ROS2 Node with Behavior Tree Execution

```python
import py_trees
import rclpy
from rclpy.node import Node
from std_msgs.msg import Float32, String
import time


def create_behavior_tree(ros_node):
    root = py_trees.composites.Selector("Root")

    # Battery check sequence
    battery_sequence =
py_trees.composites.Sequence("Battery Check")
    battery_monitor =
BatteryMonitor(ros_node=ros_node)
    navigate_to_charge =
NavigateToCharge(ros_node=ros_node)

battery_sequence.add_children([battery_monitor,
navigate_to_charge])
```

```python
    # Cleaning sequence
    cleaning_sequence =
py_trees.composites.Sequence("Cleaning")
    start_cleaning =
StartCleaning(ros_node=ros_node)
    perform_cleaning =
PerformCleaning(ros_node=ros_node)

cleaning_sequence.add_children([start_cleaning,
perform_cleaning])

    # Add sequences to root
    root.add_children([battery_sequence,
cleaning_sequence])

    return root

class BehaviorTreeNode(Node):
    def __init__(self):
        super().__init__('behavior_tree_node')
        self.behaviour_tree =
py_trees.trees.BehaviourTree(create_behavior_tree
(self))
        self.timer = self.create_timer(0.1,
self.tick_tree)

    def tick_tree(self):
        self.behaviour_tree.tick()
```

```
def main(args=None):
    rclpy.init(args=args)
    node = BehaviorTreeNode()
    try:
        rclpy.spin(node)
    except KeyboardInterrupt:
        pass
    node.destroy_node()
    rclpy.shutdown()


if __name__ == "__main__":
    main()
```

Explanation:

- **BehaviorTreeNode:** A ROS2 node that continuously ticks the Behavior Tree, allowing real-time behavior execution.

- **Timer:** Calls the tick_tree method at regular intervals (e.g., every 0.1 seconds) to update the Behavior Tree.

State Management with Python

Effective state management ensures that your robot behaves consistently and predictably. While Behavior Trees handle state implicitly through their structure, integrating explicit state management can enhance control and monitoring.

Example: Enhanced State Management

Scenario: Your robot needs to switch between different operational modes—Cleaning, Charging, and Idle—based on various conditions like battery level and task completion.

Implementation:

1. Define Operational States:

python

```python
from enum import Enum


class OperationalState(Enum):
    IDLE = 1
    CLEANING = 2
    CHARGING = 3
```

2. Implement State Management within Behavior Tree Nodes:

python

```python
class
BatteryMonitor(py_trees.behaviour.Behaviour):
    def __init__(self, name="Battery Monitor",
ros_node=None):
        super(BatteryMonitor,
self).__init__(name)
        self.ros_node = ros_node
        self.battery_level = 100.0
```

```
        self.subscription =
self.ros_node.create_subscription(
            Float32,
            'battery_level',
            self.battery_callback,
            10)
        self.subscription  # prevent unused
variable warning


    def battery_callback(self, msg):
        self.battery_level = msg.data
        self.logger.info(f'Battery level updated:
{self.battery_level}%')


    def update(self):
        if self.battery_level < 20.0:
            return py_trees.common.Status.SUCCESS
        else:
            return py_trees.common.Status.FAILURE
```

3. Use States to Influence Behavior Execution:

Modify Behavior Tree nodes to react based on the current operational state.

```python
class
CleaningSequence(py_trees.composites.Sequence):
```

```python
    def __init__(self, name="Cleaning Sequence",
ros_node=None):
        super(CleaningSequence,
self).__init__(name)
        self.ros_node = ros_node
        self.state = OperationalState.IDLE

self.add_children([StartCleaning(ros_node=ros_nod
e), PerformCleaning(ros_node=ros_node)])

    def update(self):
        if self.state ==
OperationalState.CLEANING:
            return super(CleaningSequence,
self).update()
        else:
            return py_trees.common.Status.FAILURE
```

Explanation:

- **OperationalState Enum:** Defines clear states for the robot.

- **BatteryMonitor:** Updates the battery level and triggers state changes.

- **CleaningSequence:** Executes cleaning behaviors only if the robot is in the **CLEANING** state.

Benefits:

- **Clarity:** Explicit states make behavior control easier to understand and manage.

- **Flexibility:** States can be extended or modified without altering the entire Behavior Tree structure.

- **Debugging:** Easier to trace and debug behaviors based on well-defined states.

Summary

In Chapter 7, "Behavior Control and State Machines," we explored the pivotal role of structured behavior management in robotic systems. We began by distinguishing between **State Machines** and **Behavior Trees**, highlighting their unique structures, advantages, and appropriate use cases. While State Machines offer simplicity and predictability for straightforward behaviors, Behavior Trees provide greater flexibility and scalability, making them ideal for managing complex and dynamic robotic tasks.

Delving deeper, we examined how to implement behavior control within ROS2 using the py_trees library. We learned to create custom behavior nodes, assemble them into a cohesive Behavior Tree, and integrate this tree within a ROS2 node to enable real-time behavior execution. The chapter also emphasized the importance of state management, demonstrating how to incorporate explicit states within Behavior Trees to enhance control and monitoring.

Through a comprehensive hands-on project, you designed a Behavior Tree that enabled your robot to perform cleaning tasks while autonomously monitoring its battery level and navigating to the charging station when necessary. This practical application reinforced the theoretical concepts, showcasing how to leverage ROS2 and Python to create intelligent, adaptive behaviors in robotic systems.

By mastering Behavior Control and State Machines, you've equipped your robots with the cognitive framework necessary for autonomous operation, enabling them to perform complex tasks, adapt to changing environments, and operate reliably with minimal human intervention. This chapter serves as a cornerstone in your robotics journey, paving the way for more advanced applications and sophisticated autonomous behaviors.

Chapter 8: Advanced Topics in Autonomous Robotics

Welcome to **Advanced Topics in Autonomous Robotics**, where we delve into the cutting-edge technologies that propel modern robots into realms of intelligence and collaboration previously thought unattainable. Think of this chapter as the rocket fuel for your robotic projects, integrating Machine Learning (ML) and Artificial Intelligence (AI), orchestrating multi-robot harmony, and empowering your robot with the ability to recognize and interact with its environment intelligently. Whether you're aspiring to build smarter robots or enhance existing systems, this chapter equips you with the knowledge and hands-on experience to push the boundaries of what's possible in autonomous robotics. Let's embark on this journey to elevate your robotics prowess!

Machine Learning and AI Integration

Basics of Machine Learning for Robotics

Have you ever wondered how robots can recognize objects, make decisions, or learn from their environment? The secret lies in **Machine Learning (ML)** and **Artificial Intelligence (AI).** These technologies empower robots to process data, identify patterns, and make informed decisions, transforming them from mere machines into intelligent agents.

What is Machine Learning?

At its core, **Machine Learning** is a subset of AI that enables systems to learn and improve from experience without being explicitly programmed. Instead of following fixed instructions, ML models analyze data, discern patterns, and make predictions or decisions based on that analysis.

Key ML Techniques in Robotics:

1. **Supervised Learning:**

   - **Definition:** Models are trained on labeled datasets, where each input is paired with the correct output.

   - **Applications:** Object recognition, where images are labeled with the names of the objects they contain.

2. **Unsupervised Learning:**

   - **Definition:** Models find hidden patterns or intrinsic structures in input data without labeled responses.

   - **Applications:** Clustering similar sensor readings to identify different terrains or environments.

3. **Reinforcement Learning:**

   o **Definition:** Models learn to make sequences of decisions by receiving rewards or penalties.

   o **Applications:** Path planning, where a robot learns to navigate efficiently by maximizing rewards for reaching destinations quickly and safely.

Why is ML Important in Robotics?

- **Adaptability:** Robots can adjust their behavior based on new data, making them more versatile.

- **Efficiency:** Optimizes processes like movement, energy consumption, and task execution.

- **Autonomy:** Reduces the need for constant human intervention, allowing robots to operate independently in dynamic environments.

Analogy: Imagine teaching a child to recognize different fruits. Initially, you show them labeled images (supervised learning). Over time, they start grouping similar fruits without labels (unsupervised learning) and eventually learn to pick the best path through an orchard by trial and error (reinforcement learning). Similarly, ML enables robots to learn and adapt from their experiences.

Machine Learning Techniques in Robotics

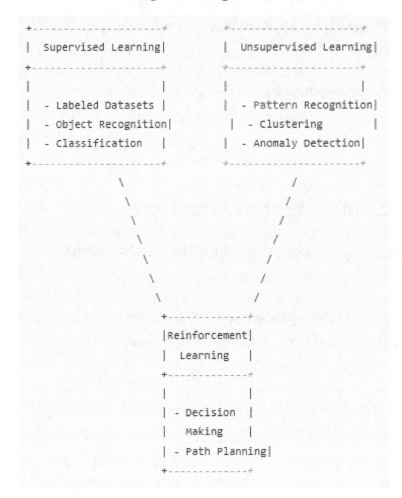

Diagram Explanation: This diagram illustrates the three primary ML techniques used in robotics, showcasing their distinct applications and how they interrelate to enhance robotic intelligence.

Implementing AI Models with ROS2 and Python

Integrating AI models into your robotic systems can seem daunting, but with **ROS2** (Robot Operating System 2) and **Python**, the process becomes manageable and efficient. ROS2 provides the communication infrastructure, while Python offers the flexibility needed to implement and manage ML models.

Step-by-Step Guide to Integrating AI Models with ROS2

Step 1: Choose the Right ML Framework

Select a framework that aligns with your project requirements. Popular choices include:

- **TensorFlow:** Known for its scalability and extensive support for various ML tasks.

- **PyTorch:** Favored for its dynamic computation graph and ease of use, especially in research.

- **scikit-learn:** Ideal for traditional ML algorithms like regression, classification, and clustering.

Step 2: Develop or Train Your Model

1. **Data Collection:**
   - Gather data relevant to your task, such as images for object recognition or sensor readings for environment mapping.

- Ensure data quality and diversity to improve model accuracy.

2. **Data Preprocessing:**

   - Clean the data by removing noise and handling missing values.

   - Normalize or scale data to ensure consistency.

3. **Model Selection:**

   - Choose an architecture suited to your task. For example, Convolutional Neural Networks (CNNs) are excellent for image-related tasks.

4. **Training:**

   - Train your model using the preprocessed data.

   - Monitor metrics like accuracy and loss to evaluate performance.

5. **Evaluation:**

   - Test your model on unseen data to assess its generalization capabilities.

   - Fine-tune hyperparameters to optimize performance.

6. **Exporting the Model:**

   - Save the trained model in a format compatible with your chosen framework (e.g., .h5 for TensorFlow).

Step 3: Create ROS2 Nodes to Load and Run the Model

1. Set Up Your ROS2 Workspace:

```bash
```

```bash
mkdir -p ~/ros2_ml_ws/src
cd ~/ros2_ml_ws/
colcon build
source install/setup.bash
```

2. Develop a Python ROS2 Node:

Create a new ROS2 package if you haven't already:

```bash
```

```bash
cd ~/ros2_ml_ws/src
ros2 pkg create --build-type ament_python
ai_integration
```

Navigate to the package directory and create a Python script:

```bash
```

```bash
cd ai_integration
mkdir ai_integration
touch ai_integration/object_recognition_node.py
chmod +x
ai_integration/object_recognition_node.py
```

Example: Object Recognition Node

```python
```

```python
#!/usr/bin/env python3
import rclpy
from rclpy.node import Node
from sensor_msgs.msg import Image
from cv_bridge import CvBridge
import tensorflow as tf
import numpy as np

class ObjectRecognitionNode(Node):
    def __init__(self):

super().__init__('object_recognition_node')
        self.subscription =
self.create_subscription(
            Image,
            'camera/image_raw',
            self.image_callback,
            10)
        self.bridge = CvBridge()
        self.model =
tf.keras.models.load_model('/path/to/your/model.h
5')
        self.publisher =
self.create_publisher(String, 'object_detection',
10)
        self.get_logger().info('Object
Recognition Node Initialized.')
```

```python
    def image_callback(self, msg):
        # Convert ROS Image message to OpenCV
image
        cv_image = self.bridge.imgmsg_to_cv2(msg,
desired_encoding='rgb8')
        # Preprocess image for model
        input_image = cv_image / 255.0   #
Normalize
        input_image = np.expand_dims(input_image,
axis=0)   # Add batch dimension
        # Run prediction
        predictions =
self.model.predict(input_image)
        # Process predictions (example: class
with highest probability)
        detected_class = np.argmax(predictions,
axis=1)[0]
        # Publish detection result
        detection_msg = String()
        detection_msg.data = f'Detected Class:
{detected_class}'
        self.publisher.publish(detection_msg)
        self.get_logger().info(f'Detected Class:
{detected_class}')

def main(args=None):
    rclpy.init(args=args)
```

```
node = ObjectRecognitionNode()
try:
    rclpy.spin(node)
except KeyboardInterrupt:
    pass
node.destroy_node()
rclpy.shutdown()


if __name__ == '__main__':
    main()
```

Explanation:

- **CvBridge:** Converts ROS image messages to OpenCV images for processing.

- **TensorFlow Model:** Loads a pre-trained TensorFlow model for object recognition.

- **Image Callback:** Processes incoming images, runs predictions, and publishes the detected class.

3. Update setup.py:

Ensure your node is discoverable by ROS2 by updating the setup.py file:

```python

from setuptools import setup


package_name = 'ai_integration'
```

```
setup(
    name=package_name,
    version='0.0.0',
    packages=[package_name],
    install_requires=['setuptools', 'tensorflow',
'cv_bridge', 'opencv-python'],
    zip_safe=True,
    maintainer='your_name',
    maintainer_email='your_email@example.com',
    description='AI Integration with ROS2',
    license='Apache License 2.0',
    tests_require=['pytest'],
    entry_points={
        'console_scripts': [
            'object_recognition_node =
ai_integration.object_recognition_node:main',
        ],
    },
)
```

4. Build the Package:

```bash
cd ~/ros2_ml_ws/
colcon build
source install/setup.bash
```

5. Run the Object Recognition Node:

bash

```
ros2 run ai_integration object_recognition_node
```

AI Model Integration with ROS2 Flowchart

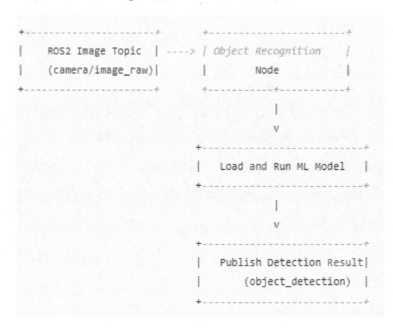

Diagram Explanation: This flowchart demonstrates how sensor data from a ROS2 image topic flows into an object recognition node, which processes the data using a machine learning model and publishes the detection results.

Best Practices for Integrating AI with ROS2

- **Modularity:** Keep AI components separate from core robot functions to enhance maintainability and scalability.

- **Resource Management:** Ensure your robot's hardware can handle the computational load of running ML models, possibly leveraging hardware accelerators like GPUs.

- **Real-Time Processing:** Optimize your ML models for real-time inference by reducing model size or using efficient architectures.

- **Continuous Learning:** Implement mechanisms for your robot to update or retrain models based on new data, enhancing adaptability.

- **Security:** Protect your AI integration from vulnerabilities by securing communication channels and validating inputs.

Multi-Robot Systems

Imagine a team of robots working in harmony, each with specialized roles, communicating seamlessly to achieve a common goal. This synergy is the essence of **Multi-Robot Systems (MRS)**, where multiple robots collaborate, share information, and coordinate actions to perform tasks more efficiently and effectively than individual robots could alone.

Coordination and Communication Between Multiple Robots

Effective coordination and communication are the lifeblood of successful Multi-Robot Systems. They ensure that robots operate cohesively, avoid conflicts, and leverage each other's strengths to accomplish complex tasks.

Key Elements:

1. **Communication Protocols:**

    ○ **ROS2's DDS (Data Distribution Service):** ROS2 utilizes DDS for real-time, scalable, and robust communication between robots. It handles message passing, service calls, and action servers/clients seamlessly.

    ○ **Wireless Technologies:** Wi-Fi, Bluetooth, and Mesh Networks facilitate connectivity between robots, ensuring reliable data transmission even in challenging environments.

2. **Coordination Strategies:**

    ○ **Centralized Coordination:**

        ▪ **Description:** A single robot or a central server manages and assigns tasks to all robots.

        ▪ **Advantages:** Simplifies decision-making and task allocation.

        ▪ **Disadvantages:** Single point of failure; scalability issues.

    ○ **Decentralized Coordination:**

        ▪ **Description:** Each robot independently makes decisions based on local information and shared data.

- **Advantages:** Enhanced scalability and robustness; no single point of failure.

- **Disadvantages:** More complex algorithms; potential for conflicts without proper protocols.

3. **Task Allocation and Load Balancing:**

   o **Dynamic Task Allocation:** Assigns tasks to robots based on their current state, capabilities, and availability.

   o **Load Balancing:** Distributes tasks evenly to prevent overburdening specific robots, optimizing overall system performance.

4. **Synchronization and Conflict Resolution:**

   o **Synchronization:** Ensures that robots operate in a coordinated manner, especially during simultaneous actions.

   o **Conflict Resolution:** Implements rules and protocols to handle competing actions or resource access, maintaining system harmony.

Analogy: Think of a team of chefs in a bustling kitchen. Each chef has a specific role (sautéing, baking, plating) and communicates with each other to ensure that dishes are prepared efficiently without stepping on each other's toes. Similarly, in an MRS, robots must communicate and coordinate their actions to perform tasks seamlessly.

Multi-Robot Communication Flowchart

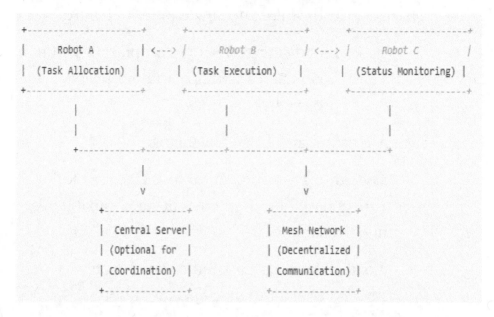

Diagram Explanation: This flowchart illustrates different communication pathways in a Multi-Robot System, highlighting both centralized and decentralized coordination strategies.

Applications of Multi-Robot Systems

Multi-Robot Systems are revolutionizing various industries by enabling scalable, efficient, and versatile operations. Here are some prominent applications:

1. **Industrial Automation:**
   - **Collaborative Manufacturing:** Multiple robots work together on assembly lines, increasing production speed and reducing errors.

- o **Warehouse Management:** Robots coordinate to manage inventory, pick and place items, and optimize storage space.

2. **Search and Rescue:**

   - o **Disaster Response:** Teams of robots navigate hazardous environments to locate and assist victims, gather data, and assess structural integrity.

   - o **Wildfire Monitoring:** Coordinated robots monitor fire spread, identify hotspots, and relay critical information to human responders.

3. **Agriculture:**

   - o **Precision Farming:** Robots collaborate to plant, monitor, and harvest crops, optimizing resource use and increasing yield.

   - o **Livestock Monitoring:** Teams of robots track animal health and movement, ensuring efficient farm management.

4. **Healthcare:**

   - o **Assisted Living:** Robots assist elderly or disabled individuals with daily tasks, enhancing independence and quality of life.

   - o **Hospital Logistics:** Coordinated robots manage supplies, transport medications, and maintain cleanliness in healthcare facilities.

5. **Environmental Monitoring:**

   ○ **Pollution Tracking:** Multi-robot systems monitor air and water quality across vast areas, providing real-time data for environmental protection.

   ○ **Wildlife Monitoring:** Robots track animal populations, migration patterns, and habitat changes to support conservation efforts.

Hands-On Project: AI-Powered Object Recognition

Ready to take your robot's intelligence to the next level? In this hands-on project, we'll guide you through creating an **AI-Powered Object Recognition** system. This project involves training a simple neural network to recognize objects and integrating it with ROS2, enabling your robot to identify and respond to objects in its environment intelligently.

Training a Simple Neural Network

Step 1: Set Up Your Development Environment

Before diving into training your neural network, ensure you have the necessary tools and libraries installed.

1. **Install Python and Pip:**

Ensure Python 3.x and pip are installed on your system.

bash

```
sudo apt update
sudo apt install python3 python3-pip
```

2. Install TensorFlow and Other Dependencies:

TensorFlow is a popular ML framework for building neural networks.

```bash
```

```
pip3 install tensorflow numpy matplotlib
```

3. Set Up a Virtual Environment (Optional but Recommended):

Virtual environments help manage dependencies and avoid conflicts.

```bash
```

```
python3 -m venv ml_env
source ml_env/bin/activate
pip install tensorflow numpy matplotlib
```

Step 2: Collect and Prepare Your Dataset

A well-prepared dataset is crucial for training an effective neural network.

1. Choose a Dataset:

For simplicity, use the **CIFAR-10** dataset, which contains 60,000 32x32 color images in 10 classes (e.g., airplanes, cars, birds).

```python
import tensorflow as tf
from tensorflow.keras.datasets import cifar10
import matplotlib.pyplot as plt

# Load CIFAR-10 dataset
(x_train, y_train), (x_test, y_test) =
cifar10.load_data()
```

2. Explore the Dataset:

Visualizing some samples helps understand the data.

```python
class_names = ['airplane', 'automobile', 'bird',
'cat', 'deer',
             'dog', 'frog', 'horse', 'ship',
'truck']

plt.figure(figsize=(10,10))
for i in range(25):
    plt.subplot(5,5,i+1)
    plt.xticks([])
    plt.yticks([])
    plt.grid(False)
    plt.imshow(x_train[i])
    plt.xlabel(class_names[y_train[i][0]])
plt.show()
```

3. Preprocess the Data:

Normalize pixel values and convert labels to categorical format.

```python
x_train, x_test = x_train / 255.0, x_test / 255.0

y_train = tf.keras.utils.to_categorical(y_train,
10)
y_test = tf.keras.utils.to_categorical(y_test,
10)
```

Step 3: Define and Train the Neural Network

1. Build the Model:

Create a simple Convolutional Neural Network (CNN) suitable for image classification.

```python
model = tf.keras.models.Sequential([
    tf.keras.layers.Conv2D(32, (3,3),
activation='relu', input_shape=(32, 32, 3)),
    tf.keras.layers.MaxPooling2D((2,2)),
    tf.keras.layers.Conv2D(64, (3,3),
activation='relu'),
    tf.keras.layers.MaxPooling2D((2,2)),
    tf.keras.layers.Conv2D(64, (3,3),
activation='relu'),
```

```python
    tf.keras.layers.Flatten(),
    tf.keras.layers.Dense(64, activation='relu'),
    tf.keras.layers.Dense(10,
activation='softmax')
])
```

2. Compile the Model:

Specify the optimizer, loss function, and metrics.

python

```python
model.compile(optimizer='adam',
          loss='categorical_crossentropy',
          metrics=['accuracy'])
```

3. Train the Model:

Fit the model to the training data.

python

```python
history = model.fit(x_train, y_train, epochs=10,
              validation_data=(x_test,
y_test))
```

4. Evaluate the Model:

Assess the model's performance on the test dataset.

python

```python
test_loss, test_acc = model.evaluate(x_test,
y_test, verbose=2)
print(f'Test accuracy: {test_acc}')
```

5. **Save the Trained Model:**

Export the model for later use in ROS2.

```python

model.save('cifar10_model.h5')
```

Best Practices for Training Neural Networks

- **Data Augmentation:** Enhance the diversity of your training data by applying random transformations like rotations, flips, and shifts.

- **Regularization:** Prevent overfitting by adding techniques like dropout or L2 regularization.

- **Early Stopping:** Halt training when validation performance stops improving to avoid overfitting.

- **Model Checkpointing:** Save the best-performing model during training for future use.

- **Hyperparameter Tuning:** Experiment with different learning rates, batch sizes, and network architectures to optimize performance.

Integrating Object Recognition with ROS2

Now that you have a trained neural network for object recognition, it's time to integrate it with ROS2, enabling your robot to identify and respond to objects in real-time.

Step-by-Step Integration Guide

Step 1: Prepare Your ROS2 Environment

1. **Ensure ROS2 is Installed:**

Follow the official ROS2 installation guide to set up ROS2 (e.g., Humble Hawksbill).

2. **Create a ROS2 Workspace:**

bash

```
mkdir -p ~/ros2_ml_ws/src
cd ~/ros2_ml_ws/
colcon build
source install/setup.bash
```

Step 2: Develop the Object Recognition ROS2 Node

1. **Create a New ROS2 Package:**

bash

```
cd ~/ros2_ml_ws/src
ros2 pkg create --build-type ament_python
ai_object_recognition
```

2. **Navigate to the Package Directory:**

bash

```
cd ai_object_recognition
```

```
mkdir ai_object_recognition
touch
ai_object_recognition/object_recognition_node.py
chmod +x
ai_object_recognition/object_recognition_node.py
```

3. Implement the Object Recognition Node:

python

```python
#!/usr/bin/env python3
import rclpy
from rclpy.node import Node
from sensor_msgs.msg import Image
from std_msgs.msg import String
from cv_bridge import CvBridge
import tensorflow as tf
import numpy as np
import cv2

class ObjectRecognitionNode(Node):
    def __init__(self):

super().__init__('object_recognition_node')
        self.subscription =
self.create_subscription(
            Image,
            'camera/image_raw',
            self.image_callback,
            10)
```

```python
        self.publisher =
self.create_publisher(String, 'object_detection',
10)
        self.bridge = CvBridge()
        self.model =
tf.keras.models.load_model('/path/to/cifar10_mode
l.h5')  # Update the path
        self.class_names = ['airplane',
'automobile', 'bird', 'cat', 'deer',
                            'dog', 'frog',
'horse', 'ship', 'truck']
        self.get_logger().info('Object
Recognition Node Initialized.')


    def image_callback(self, msg):
        # Convert ROS Image message to OpenCV
image
        cv_image = self.bridge.imgmsg_to_cv2(msg,
desired_encoding='rgb8')
        # Resize image to 32x32 as per CIFAR-10
        resized_image = cv2.resize(cv_image, (32,
32))
        # Normalize image
        input_image = resized_image / 255.0
        input_image = np.expand_dims(input_image,
axis=0)  # Add batch dimension
        # Predict
```

```python
        predictions =
self.model.predict(input_image)
        detected_class =
self.class_names[np.argmax(predictions,
axis=1)[0]]
        confidence = np.max(predictions,
axis=1)[0]
        # Publish detection result
        detection_msg = String()
        detection_msg.data = f'Detected Class:
{detected_class} (Confidence:
{confidence*100:.2f}%)'
        self.publisher.publish(detection_msg)
        self.get_logger().info(f'Detected Class:
{detected_class} (Confidence:
{confidence*100:.2f}%)')


def main(args=None):
    rclpy.init(args=args)
    node = ObjectRecognitionNode()
    try:
        rclpy.spin(node)
    except KeyboardInterrupt:
        pass
    node.destroy_node()
    rclpy.shutdown()


if __name__ == '__main__':
```

```
main()
```

Explanation:

- **CvBridge:** Converts ROS image messages to OpenCV images.

- **TensorFlow Model:** Loads the trained CIFAR-10 model for object recognition.

- **Image Callback:** Processes incoming images, resizes them to match the model's input, runs predictions, and publishes the detection results.

4. **Update setup.py:**

Edit the setup.py file to include your node:

```python

from setuptools import setup


package_name = 'ai_object_recognition'


setup(
    name=package_name,
    version='0.0.0',
    packages=[package_name],
    install_requires=['setuptools', 'tensorflow',
'cv_bridge', 'opencv-python'],
    zip_safe=True,
    maintainer='your_name',
    maintainer_email='your_email@example.com',
```

```
    description='AI-Powered Object Recognition
with ROS2',
    license='Apache License 2.0',
    tests_require=['pytest'],
    entry_points={
        'console_scripts': [
            'object_recognition_node =
ai_object_recognition.object_recognition_node:mai
n',
        ],
    },
)
```

5. **Build the Package:**

```bash

cd ~/ros2_ml_ws/
colcon build
source install/setup.bash
```

Step 3: Launch the Object Recognition System

1. **Run the Object Recognition Node:**

```bash

ros2 run ai_object_recognition
object_recognition_node
```

2. **Simulate or Use a Real Camera Feed:**

If you don't have a real camera, you can use ROS2's image_tools package to publish sample images.

bash

```bash
sudo apt install ros-humble-image-tools
ros2 run image_tools cam2image --ros-args -p
frequency:=1
```

3. **Monitor Detection Results:**

In another terminal, subscribe to the object_detection topic to see the detection results.

bash

```bash
ros2 topic echo /object_detection
```

Expected Output:

kotlin

```kotlin
data: "Detected Class: airplane (Confidence:
85.50%)"
```

Object Recognition Integration Flowchart

```
+--------------------+        +----------------------+        +----------------------+
|                    |        |                      |        |                      |
|   Camera Feed      | ----> | Object Recognition   | ----> | Detection Publisher  |
|                    |        |                      |        |                      |
| (camera/image_raw) |        |    Node (ROS2)       |        | (object_detection)   |
|                    |        |                      |        |                      |
+--------------------+        +----------------------+        +----------------------+
```

Diagram Explanation: This flowchart illustrates the data flow from the camera feed to the object recognition node and finally to the detection publisher, enabling real-time object recognition within ROS2.

Best Practices for AI Integration in Robotics

- **Optimize Model Performance:**
  - Reduce model size using techniques like pruning or quantization to enable faster inference on resource-constrained robots.
  - Utilize hardware accelerators like GPUs or TPUs if available.

- **Ensure Real-Time Processing:**
  - Implement asynchronous processing to prevent blocking critical robot operations.
  - Use multi-threading or multi-processing to handle sensor data and AI computations concurrently.

- **Handle Edge Cases:**
  - Anticipate and manage scenarios where the model might fail or produce low-confidence predictions.
  - Implement fallback behaviors to ensure robot safety and reliability.

- **Maintain Model Updates:**

- Continuously retrain and update models with new data to improve accuracy and adaptability.

- Implement version control for models to track changes and revert if necessary.

- **Secure AI Systems:**

    - Protect your models and data from unauthorized access and tampering.

    - Validate and sanitize all inputs to prevent injection attacks or erroneous behavior.

Multi-Robot Systems

Coordination and Communication Between Multiple Robots

Imagine a swarm of drones efficiently mapping a disaster area, each contributing unique data while avoiding collisions and redundancies. This level of coordination and communication is the hallmark of **Multi-Robot Systems (MRS),** where multiple robots work in unison to achieve objectives that would be impossible or inefficient for a single robot to accomplish alone.

Understanding Coordination in MRS

Coordination in MRS refers to the organized interaction between robots to perform tasks collectively. Effective coordination ensures that each robot operates optimally within the system, leveraging its strengths while compensating for others.

Key Coordination Strategies:

1. **Task Allocation:**

   o **Static Allocation:** Predefined tasks assigned to specific robots.

   o **Dynamic Allocation:** Tasks are distributed based on real-time conditions, robot availability, and capabilities.

2. **Resource Sharing:**

   o **Shared Sensors:** Multiple robots can share sensor data to enhance environmental understanding.

   o **Shared Tools:** Robots can utilize tools or equipment owned by others, optimizing resource usage.

3. **Collaborative Mapping:**

   o Robots contribute to a shared map, pooling their sensor data to create a comprehensive environmental model.

4. **Load Balancing:**

   o Distributes tasks evenly among robots to prevent overburdening and ensure efficient operation.

Communication Mechanisms in MRS

Robots in an MRS communicate through various means, each with its own advantages and considerations:

1. **ROS2's DDS (Data Distribution Service):**

   o **Description:** A middleware protocol used by ROS2 for communication between nodes.

   o **Advantages:** Real-time data exchange, scalability, and support for multiple communication paradigms (publish/subscribe, services, actions).

2. **Wireless Technologies:**

   o **Wi-Fi:** Offers high bandwidth and range, suitable for indoor and urban environments.

   o **Bluetooth:** Ideal for short-range, low-power communication.

   o **Mesh Networks:** Enable robust, self-healing communication paths, enhancing reliability in dynamic environments.

3. **Communication Protocols:**

   o **Publish/Subscribe:** Enables decoupled communication where robots publish data to topics that others subscribe to.

- Peer-to-Peer: Direct communication between robots for specific tasks like resource sharing or coordination.

Applications of Multi-Robot Systems

Multi-Robot Systems are transforming industries by enabling scalable, efficient, and versatile operations. Here are some key applications:

1. Industrial Automation:

   - Collaborative Manufacturing: Robots work together on assembly lines, performing tasks like welding, painting, and packaging with precision and speed.

   - Warehouse Management: Teams of robots manage inventory, handle order fulfillment, and optimize storage space, enhancing productivity and reducing errors.

2. Search and Rescue:

   - Disaster Response: Multiple robots navigate through rubble, locate survivors, and assess structural damage, providing critical information to human responders.

   - Wildfire Monitoring: Coordinated robots monitor fire spread, detect hotspots, and relay data for effective firefighting strategies.

3. Agriculture:

- o **Precision Farming:** Robots collaborate to plant seeds, monitor crop health, and harvest produce, optimizing resource use and increasing yield.

- o **Livestock Monitoring:** Teams of robots track animal movements, monitor health indicators, and manage farm operations efficiently.

4. **Healthcare:**

- o **Assisted Living:** Multiple robots assist elderly or disabled individuals with daily tasks, enhancing their independence and quality of life.

- o **Hospital Logistics:** Robots coordinate to manage supplies, transport medications, and maintain cleanliness, improving hospital efficiency.

5. **Environmental Monitoring:**

- o **Pollution Tracking:** Multi-robot systems monitor air and water quality across vast areas, providing real-time data for environmental protection.

- o **Wildlife Monitoring:** Teams of robots track animal populations, migration patterns, and habitat changes to support conservation efforts.

Coordination and Communication Techniques

1. **Consensus Algorithms:**

   o **Definition:** Algorithms that enable robots to agree on certain states or decisions despite potential communication delays or failures.

   o **Examples:** Distributed consensus algorithms like Paxos or Raft used for synchronized task execution.

2. **Formation Control:**

   o **Description:** Strategies that maintain specific formations (e.g., line, circle) among multiple robots.

   o **Applications:** Search and rescue operations where formations help cover areas systematically.

3. **Task Allocation Mechanisms:**

   o **Market-Based Allocation:** Robots bid for tasks based on their capabilities and current state.

   o **Role-Based Allocation:** Assigning specific roles to robots (e.g., scout, helper) based on predefined criteria.

4. **Swarm Intelligence:**

- o **Concept:** Inspired by natural systems like ant colonies or bee swarms, where simple rules lead to complex, emergent behaviors.

- o **Applications:** Coordinated exploration, collective mapping, and adaptive task distribution.

Implementing Coordination in ROS2

ROS2 provides a robust framework for implementing coordination and communication in Multi-Robot Systems. Leveraging ROS2's features, you can design systems where robots interact, share information, and collaborate seamlessly.

Step-by-Step Guide to Implementing Coordination

Step 1: Set Up Your ROS2 Environment for Multi-Robot Communication

1. **Ensure All Robots Are Connected to the Same Network:**

This facilitates seamless communication between robots using ROS2's DDS-based system.

2. **Configure ROS2 Networking:**

   - o Set unique ROS_DOMAIN_ID for separate robot networks or the same ID for a unified network.

o Ensure firewalls or network policies allow ROS2 traffic.

Step 2: Implement Communication Nodes

1. Create Publisher and Subscriber Nodes:

Robots can publish their status, sensor data, or task updates to shared topics that other robots subscribe to.

Example: Status Publisher Node

python

```python
# status_publisher.py
import rclpy
from rclpy.node import Node
from std_msgs.msg import String
import time


class StatusPublisher(Node):
    def __init__(self, robot_id):
        super().__init__('status_publisher')
        self.publisher =
self.create_publisher(String, 'robot_status', 10)
        self.timer = self.create_timer(1.0,
self.publish_status)
        self.robot_id = robot_id

    def publish_status(self):
        msg = String()
```

```python
        msg.data = f'Robot {self.robot_id}
Status: Active'
        self.publisher.publish(msg)
        self.get_logger().info(f'Publishing:
{msg.data}')


def main(args=None):
    rclpy.init(args=args)
    robot_id = 'A'  # Change as per robot
    node = StatusPublisher(robot_id)
    try:
        rclpy.spin(node)
    except KeyboardInterrupt:
        pass
    node.destroy_node()
    rclpy.shutdown()


if __name__ == '__main__':
    main()
```

2. Create Coordinator Nodes (Optional):

If using a centralized approach, a coordinator node can manage task allocation and communication.

Example: Task Coordinator Node

```python
python


# task_coordinator.py
import rclpy
```

```python
from rclpy.node import Node
from std_msgs.msg import String


class TaskCoordinator(Node):
    def __init__(self):
        super().__init__('task_coordinator')
        self.subscription =
self.create_subscription(
            String,
            'robot_status',
            self.status_callback,
            10)
        self.task_publisher =
self.create_publisher(String, 'task_assignment',
10)
        self.get_logger().info('Task Coordinator
Node Initialized.')


    def status_callback(self, msg):
        self.get_logger().info(f'Received Status:
{msg.data}')
        # Simple task allocation logic
        if 'Active' in msg.data:
            task_msg = String()
            task_msg.data = 'Task: Clean Area 1'
            self.task_publisher.publish(task_msg)
            self.get_logger().info(f'Assigned
Task: {task_msg.data}')
```

```
def main(args=None):
    rclpy.init(args=args)
    node = TaskCoordinator()
    try:
        rclpy.spin(node)
    except KeyboardInterrupt:
        pass
    node.destroy_node()
    rclpy.shutdown()


if __name__ == '__main__':
    main()
```

Step 3: Implement Coordination Logic

1. Define Task Allocation Rules:

Determine how tasks are assigned based on robot status, capabilities, and current load.

2. Implement Shared Knowledge Bases:

Use topics, services, or actions to share maps, sensor data, and task assignments.

3. Ensure Synchronization:

Implement mechanisms to synchronize tasks and prevent conflicts, such as two robots attempting to clean the same area.

Step 4: Test and Validate Coordination

1. **Simulate Multiple Robots:**

Use simulation tools like Gazebo to emulate multiple robots and test coordination algorithms without physical hardware.

2. **Monitor Communication:**

Utilize ROS2's tools like ros2 topic echo and ros2 graph to monitor communication and ensure messages are correctly transmitted and received.

3. **Debug and Optimize:**

Identify and resolve issues related to message delays, data consistency, and task allocation inefficiencies.

Applications of Multi-Robot Systems

Multi-Robot Systems are revolutionizing various industries by enabling scalable, efficient, and versatile operations. Let's explore some prominent applications:

1. **Industrial Automation:**

   - **Collaborative Manufacturing:** Robots work together on assembly lines, performing tasks like welding, painting, and packaging with precision and speed.

   - **Warehouse Management:** Teams of robots manage inventory, handle order fulfillment, and optimize storage space, enhancing productivity and reducing errors.

2. **Search and Rescue:**

   o **Disaster Response:** Multiple robots navigate through rubble, locate survivors, and assess structural damage, providing critical information to human responders.

   o **Wildfire Monitoring:** Coordinated robots monitor fire spread, detect hotspots, and relay data for effective firefighting strategies.

3. **Agriculture:**

   o **Precision Farming:** Robots collaborate to plant seeds, monitor crop health, and harvest produce, optimizing resource use and increasing yield.

   o **Livestock Monitoring:** Teams of robots track animal movements, monitor health indicators, and manage farm operations efficiently.

4. **Healthcare:**

   o **Assisted Living:** Multiple robots assist elderly or disabled individuals with daily tasks, enhancing independence and quality of life.

   o **Hospital Logistics:** Coordinated robots manage supplies, transport medications, and maintain cleanliness in healthcare facilities, improving hospital efficiency.

5. **Environmental Monitoring:**

- o **Pollution Tracking:** Multi-robot systems monitor air and water quality across vast areas, providing real-time data for environmental protection.

- o **Wildlife Monitoring:** Teams of robots track animal populations, migration patterns, and habitat changes to support conservation efforts.

Best Practices for Training Neural Networks

- **Data Augmentation:** Enhance the diversity of your training data by applying random transformations like rotations, flips, and shifts. This helps the model generalize better.

```python
from tensorflow.keras.preprocessing.image import ImageDataGenerator

datagen = ImageDataGenerator(
    rotation_range=15,
    horizontal_flip=True,
    width_shift_range=0.1,
    height_shift_range=0.1
)
datagen.fit(x_train)
```

- **Regularization:** Prevent overfitting by adding techniques like dropout or L2 regularization.

```python
python
```

```python
model = tf.keras.models.Sequential([
    tf.keras.layers.Conv2D(32, (3,3),
activation='relu', input_shape=(32, 32, 3)),
    tf.keras.layers.MaxPooling2D((2,2)),
    tf.keras.layers.Dropout(0.25),
    tf.keras.layers.Conv2D(64, (3,3),
activation='relu'),
    tf.keras.layers.MaxPooling2D((2,2)),
    tf.keras.layers.Dropout(0.25),
    tf.keras.layers.Conv2D(64, (3,3),
activation='relu'),
    tf.keras.layers.Flatten(),
    tf.keras.layers.Dense(64, activation='relu'),
    tf.keras.layers.Dropout(0.5),
    tf.keras.layers.Dense(10,
activation='softmax')
])
```

- **Early Stopping:** Halt training when validation performance stops improving to avoid overfitting.

```python
python
```

```python
from tensorflow.keras.callbacks import
EarlyStopping

early_stopping =
EarlyStopping(monitor='val_loss', patience=3)
```

```python
history = model.fit(x_train, y_train, epochs=10,
                    validation_data=(x_test,
y_test),
                    callbacks=[early_stopping])
```

- **Model Checkpointing:** Save the best-performing model during training.

python

```python
from tensorflow.keras.callbacks import
ModelCheckpoint

checkpoint = ModelCheckpoint('best_model.h5',
monitor='val_accuracy', save_best_only=True)
history = model.fit(x_train, y_train, epochs=10,
                    validation_data=(x_test,
y_test),
                    callbacks=[checkpoint])
```

- **Hyperparameter Tuning:** Experiment with different learning rates, batch sizes, and network architectures to optimize performance.

python

```python
optimizer =
tf.keras.optimizers.Adam(learning_rate=0.001)
model.compile(optimizer=optimizer,
              loss='categorical_crossentropy',
              metrics=['accuracy'])
```

Conclusion

Congratulations! You've successfully navigated through the intricate world of **Advanced Topics in Autonomous Robotics**, mastering the integration of Machine Learning and AI, orchestrating multi-robot coordination, and empowering your robot with intelligent object recognition capabilities. By understanding and implementing these advanced technologies, you've transformed your robotic projects from simple, reactive machines into sophisticated, autonomous agents capable of complex decision-making and collaboration.

Key Takeaways:

1. **Machine Learning and AI Integration:**

   o Grasped the basics of Machine Learning and its significance in enhancing robotic intelligence.

   o Learned how to train and integrate neural networks with ROS2 using Python, enabling real-time object recognition.

2. **Multi-Robot Systems:**

   o Explored coordination and communication strategies essential for effective collaboration among multiple robots.

   o Implemented communication protocols and coordination algorithms using ROS2, facilitating seamless task allocation and execution.

3. **Hands-On Projects:**

   o Successfully trained a neural network for object recognition and integrated it into a ROS2 environment.

   o Designed and implemented a Multi-Robot Coordination system, showcasing dynamic task allocation based on robot statuses.

Next Steps:

1. **Deepen Your ML and AI Knowledge:**

   o Explore more complex neural network architectures like Convolutional Neural Networks (CNNs) and Recurrent Neural Networks (RNNs).

   o Delve into reinforcement learning for advanced decision-making capabilities.

2. **Enhance Multi-Robot Coordination:**

   o Implement more sophisticated coordination algorithms like consensus-based methods or swarm intelligence.

   o Experiment with decentralized coordination for increased scalability and robustness.

3. **Expand to Real-World Deployments:**

   o Test your AI-powered object recognition system and Multi-Robot Coordination in real-world scenarios, identifying and addressing practical challenges.

- ○ Optimize system performance based on field observations and feedback.

4. **Incorporate Additional Sensors and Actuators:**

- ○ Integrate more diverse sensors (e.g., LIDAR, GPS) and actuators to enrich your robot's perception and interaction capabilities.

- ○ Utilize sensor fusion techniques to combine data from multiple sources for enhanced accuracy.

5. **Implement Security Measures:**

- ○ Protect your robotic systems from cyber threats by implementing secure communication channels and robust authentication mechanisms.

- ○ Ensure data integrity and confidentiality in all AI and MRS operations.

Remember: The journey into autonomous robotics is ever-evolving, with new technologies and methodologies emerging regularly. Stay curious, continuously experiment, and embrace the challenges as opportunities to innovate and refine your robotic systems.

You're now well-equipped to develop intelligent, collaborative, and autonomous robots that can navigate and interact with the world intelligently! Harness the power of Machine Learning, AI, and Multi-Robot Coordination to create sophisticated robotic solutions that can tackle complex tasks with efficiency and precision.

Summary

In Chapter 8, "Advanced Topics in Autonomous Robotics," we explored the integration of **Machine Learning (ML)** and **Artificial Intelligence (AI)** into robotic systems, enhancing their intelligence and adaptability. We delved into the basics of ML for robotics, including key techniques like supervised, unsupervised, and reinforcement learning, and demonstrated how to implement AI models within ROS2 using Python. This integration empowers robots with capabilities such as object recognition, decision-making, and real-time data processing.

The chapter further delved into **Multi-Robot Systems (MRS)**, highlighting the importance of coordination and communication among multiple robots. We examined various coordination strategies, including centralized, decentralized, and hybrid approaches, and discussed the communication mechanisms essential for effective collaboration. Applications of **MRS** across industries like industrial automation, search and rescue, agriculture, healthcare, and environmental monitoring were showcased, illustrating the versatility and impact of collaborative robotics.

Through a comprehensive hands-on project, you trained a simple neural network for object recognition and integrated it with ROS2, enabling your robot to identify objects in real-time. Additionally, you designed and implemented a Multi-Robot Coordination system, facilitating dynamic task allocation based on robot statuses and enhancing operational efficiency.

By mastering these advanced topics, you've equipped yourself with the knowledge and practical skills to develop intelligent, collaborative, and autonomous robotic systems capable of performing complex tasks with precision and efficiency. This chapter serves as a crucial milestone in your robotics journey, paving the way for more sophisticated applications and innovations in the field of autonomous robotics.

Chapter 9: Real-World Applications and Case Studies

Welcome to **Real-World Applications and Case Studies**, where theory meets practice in the dynamic landscape of autonomous robotics. Have you ever marveled at the precision of robotic arms in factories, the compassionate assistance of healthcare robots, or the relentless efficiency of delivery drones? These aren't scenes from a futuristic movie—they are the reality today, thanks to advancements in autonomous robotics. This chapter takes you on a journey through various industries, showcasing how robots are revolutionizing operations, enhancing precision, and transforming lives. Through detailed case studies, we'll uncover the practical implementations and profound impacts of robotics in manufacturing, healthcare, logistics, and space exploration. Ready to see robots in action? Let's dive in!

Manufacturing

Automation and Precision in Production Lines

Have you ever wondered how modern factories achieve such high levels of efficiency and consistency? The secret lies in the seamless integration of robotics into production lines. **Automation** in manufacturing utilizes robots to perform repetitive, precise, and often hazardous tasks, thereby enhancing productivity, reducing errors, and ensuring worker safety.

Benefits of Robotics in Manufacturing

1. **Increased Efficiency:**

   o Robots can operate continuously without fatigue, significantly speeding up production processes.

2. **Enhanced Precision:**

   o Robots perform tasks with high accuracy, ensuring consistency in product quality.

3. **Improved Safety:**

   o Robots handle dangerous tasks, minimizing the risk of workplace injuries.

4. **Cost Reduction:**

   o Automation reduces labor costs and minimizes waste, contributing to overall cost savings.

5. **Flexibility:**

- o Modern robots can be reprogrammed and reconfigured to handle different tasks, allowing for adaptability in production.

Key Areas of Robotics in Manufacturing

1. **Assembly:**

- o Robots assemble components with high precision, often performing tasks faster and more accurately than human workers.

2. **Material Handling:**

- o Automated guided vehicles (AGVs) transport materials across the factory floor, optimizing workflow and reducing manual handling.

3. **Quality Control:**

- o Robots equipped with sensors and cameras inspect products for defects, ensuring only high-quality items proceed down the production line.

4. **Packaging:**

- o Automated packaging systems wrap, box, and palletize products efficiently, speeding up the final stages of production.

Analogy: *Think of a robotic assembly line as a symphony orchestra. Each robot, like a musician, has a specific role,* *and together they create a harmonious and efficient production process.*

Automation Workflow in a Manufacturing Production Line

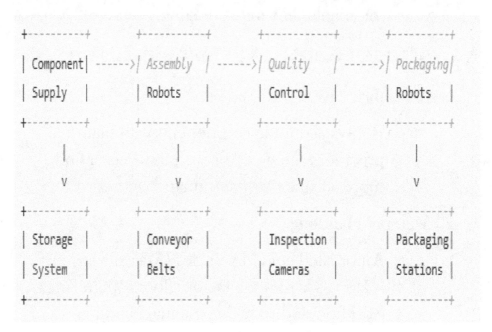

Diagram Explanation: This flowchart illustrates the automation process in a manufacturing production line, showcasing the flow from component supply to assembly, quality control, and packaging stages.

Case Study: Robotic Arms in Assembly

Let's explore a real-world example of how robotic arms have transformed assembly lines in the automotive industry.

Background

The automotive industry is renowned for its complexity and demand for precision. Traditional assembly lines rely heavily on manual labor, which can be time-consuming, inconsistent, and prone to errors. To address these challenges, major automotive manufacturers have integrated robotic arms into their assembly lines.

Implementation

1. **Selection of Robotic Arms:**

   o **KUKA Robotics** and **ABB** are among the leading manufacturers supplying robotic arms for automotive assembly.

2. **Integration into the Production Line:**

   o Robotic arms are strategically placed at critical points in the assembly line to handle tasks such as welding, painting, and component installation.

3. **Programming and Customization:**

   o Each robotic arm is programmed to perform specific tasks with high precision. Custom end-effectors are designed to handle different components seamlessly.

4. **Collaborative Robots (Cobots):**

   o To enhance flexibility, collaborative robots work alongside human workers, assisting with tasks that require both precision and human dexterity.

Outcomes

1. **Increased Productivity:**

- o Robotic arms operate faster than human workers, completing tasks more quickly and increasing overall production rates.

2. **Enhanced Quality:**

   - o The precision of robotic arms ensures consistent quality in welding and painting, reducing defects and rework.

3. **Improved Worker Safety:**

   - o Dangerous tasks, such as welding, are delegated to robots, minimizing the risk of workplace injuries.

4. **Cost Savings:**

   - o Although the initial investment in robotic arms is substantial, the long-term savings from reduced labor costs and increased efficiency justify the expense.

Challenges and Solutions

1. **Initial Investment:**

   - o **Challenge:** High upfront costs of purchasing and integrating robotic arms.

   - o **Solution:** Manufacturers offset costs by gradually introducing robots, starting with the most repetitive and hazardous tasks.

2. **Training and Skill Development:**

- ○ **Challenge:** Workforce needs to adapt to working alongside robots.

- ○ **Solution:** Comprehensive training programs are implemented to equip workers with the skills to operate and maintain robotic systems.

3. **Maintenance and Downtime:**

- ○ **Challenge:** Ensuring robotic arms are maintained to prevent downtime.

- ○ **Solution:** Predictive maintenance strategies and regular inspections are employed to keep robots running smoothly

Robotic Arm Integration in Automotive Assembly

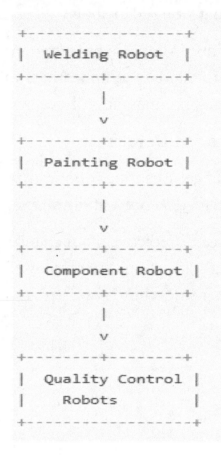

```
+------------------+
|  Welding Robot   |
+--------+---------+
         |
         v
+--------+---------+
|  Painting Robot  |
+--------+---------+
         |
         v
+--------+---------+
| Component Robot  |
+--------+---------+
         |
         v
+--------+---------+
| Quality Control  |
|    Robots        |
+------------------+
```

Diagram Explanation: This diagram showcases the integration of robotic arms in different stages of automotive assembly, from welding and painting to component installation and quality control.

Future Prospects

The use of robotic arms in assembly is poised to grow with advancements in AI and machine learning. Future developments include:

1. **Enhanced Autonomy:**

   o Robotic arms with greater autonomy can adapt to changing tasks and environments without extensive reprogramming.

2. **AI-Driven Optimization:**

   o AI algorithms analyze production data to optimize robotic arm performance, improving efficiency and reducing waste.

3. **Human-Robot Collaboration:**

   o Improved collaborative robots can work more seamlessly with human workers, combining the strengths of both to achieve superior results.

Conclusion of Case Study:

The integration of robotic arms in automotive assembly lines exemplifies the transformative power of robotics in manufacturing. By enhancing precision, productivity, and safety, robotic arms have become indispensable in modern production environments, setting the stage for future innovations and advancements.

Healthcare

Assistive Robots and Surgical Automation

Have you ever considered how robots can enhance the quality of healthcare? From assisting in daily tasks for the elderly to performing precise surgical procedures, robots are becoming invaluable allies in the medical field. **Assistive Robots** and **Surgical Automation** are two key areas where robotics is making significant strides, improving patient outcomes and streamlining healthcare operations.

Assistive Robots

Assistive robots are designed to support individuals with disabilities, the elderly, or those recovering from injuries. These robots help with daily activities, providing companionship, enhancing mobility, and ensuring safety.

Key Functions of Assistive Robots:

1. **Mobility Assistance:**

   o Robots like exoskeletons help individuals with mobility impairments to walk and perform physical tasks.

2. **Daily Task Support:**

   o Robots assist with activities such as feeding, dressing, and housekeeping, promoting independence.

3. **Companionship:**

- o Social robots provide emotional support, engage in conversations, and monitor the well-being of users.

4. **Monitoring and Alerting:**

- o Robots equipped with sensors monitor vital signs and alert caregivers in case of emergencies.

Analogy: Imagine having a personal assistant who never tires, can help you with every step you take, and always keeps an eye on your well-being. That's essentially what assistive robots offer.

Surgical Automation

Surgical robots are transforming the landscape of medical procedures, enabling surgeons to perform complex operations with greater precision, flexibility, and control.

Key Features of Surgical Robots:

1. **Enhanced Precision:**

- o Surgical robots can execute movements with micrometer precision, reducing the risk of errors.

2. **Minimally Invasive Procedures:**

- o Robots facilitate minimally invasive surgeries, resulting in smaller incisions, reduced pain, and quicker recovery times.

3. **Remote Surgery:**

- o Surgeons can perform operations remotely, expanding access to specialized care in underserved areas.

4. **Integration with Imaging:**

- o Robots can integrate with imaging systems like MRI and CT scans, providing real-time data during surgery.

Functions of Assistive and Surgical Robots in Healthcare

```
+-----------------------------+    +-------------------------------+
|     Assistive Robots    |    |      Surgical Robots        |
+-----------------------------+    +-------------------------------+
| - Mobility Assistance   |    | - Enhanced Precision        |
| - Daily Task Support    |    | - Minimally Invasive Proc.  |
| - Companionship         |    | - Remote Surgery            |
| - Monitoring and Alerting |  | - Integration with Imaging  |
+-----------------------------+    +-------------------------------+
```

Diagram Explanation: This diagram contrasts the key functions of assistive robots and surgical robots in healthcare, highlighting their unique contributions to patient care.

Case Study: Rehabilitation Robotics

Rehabilitation robotics is a burgeoning field where robots assist patients in recovering from injuries or surgeries, enhancing traditional therapy methods with precision and adaptability.

Background

Rehabilitation after injuries, strokes, or surgeries often requires intensive physical therapy. Traditional therapy can be time-consuming, and progress varies among patients. Rehabilitation robots aim to provide consistent, personalized therapy, accelerating recovery and improving outcomes.

Implementation

1. **Types of Rehabilitation Robots:**

   - **Exoskeletons:**

     - Assist patients in walking by providing support and guiding limb movements.

   - **Therapeutic Robots:**

     - Aid in exercises like arm raises, leg movements, and balance training.

   - **Virtual Reality (VR) Integration:**

     - Combine robotics with VR to create engaging and interactive therapy sessions.

2. **Key Technologies:**

- Sensors and Actuators:
  - Measure patient movements and provide the necessary force to assist or resist movements.

- Control Systems:
  - Algorithms that adapt to the patient's progress, adjusting the level of assistance dynamically.

- Data Analytics:
  - Collect and analyze movement data to tailor therapy programs and track progress.

3. Patient Interaction:
  - Patients interact with robots through intuitive interfaces, receiving real-time feedback and motivation during therapy sessions.

Outcomes

1. Improved Recovery Rates:
  - Patients experience faster and more consistent recovery due to personalized and intensive therapy.

2. Enhanced Engagement:

- o Interactive therapy sessions using **VR** and robotics make rehabilitation more engaging, increasing patient adherence.

3. **Data-Driven Insights:**

   - o Continuous data collection provides therapists with detailed insights into patient progress, enabling more informed treatment decisions.

4. **Reduced Therapist Workload:**

   - o Robots handle repetitive tasks, allowing therapists to focus on more complex and individualized aspects of care.

Challenges and Solutions

1. **High Cost:**

   - o **Challenge:** Rehabilitation robots are expensive, limiting accessibility.

   - o **Solution:** Innovations in design and manufacturing are gradually reducing costs, making robots more affordable for healthcare facilities.

2. **User Adaptation:**

   - o **Challenge:** Patients may find it challenging to adapt to robotic assistance.

- o **Solution:** User-friendly interfaces and gradual introduction to robotic assistance enhance comfort and adaptability.

3. **Integration with Existing Therapies:**

- o **Challenge:** Ensuring that robotic therapy complements rather than replaces traditional methods.

- o **Solution:** Hybrid therapy approaches that combine robotics with human-guided therapy offer the best outcomes.

Future Prospects

Rehabilitation robotics continues to evolve with advancements in AI, materials science, and human-robot interaction. Future developments include:

1. **AI-Enhanced Adaptability:**

- o Robots that learn from patient movements and adapt therapy in real-time for optimal recovery.

2. **Lightweight and Wearable Designs:**

- o More comfortable and less intrusive robotic devices that patients can wear during daily activities.

3. **Tele-rehabilitation:**

o Robots that facilitate remote therapy sessions, expanding access to rehabilitation services in remote or underserved areas.

4. **Personalized Therapy Programs:**

o Leveraging machine learning to create highly personalized therapy plans based on individual patient data.

Conclusion of Case Study:

Rehabilitation robotics exemplifies the transformative potential of robotics in healthcare. By providing consistent, personalized, and engaging therapy, robots significantly enhance patient recovery processes, offering a glimpse into a future where technology and human care work hand-in-hand to improve health outcomes.

Logistics

Autonomous Warehousing and Delivery Robots

In an era where e-commerce is booming and consumer expectations are soaring, the logistics industry is under immense pressure to deliver goods quickly and efficiently. Enter **Autonomous Warehousing and Delivery Robots**—the silent heroes revolutionizing how goods are stored, managed, and delivered.

Importance of Robotics in Logistics

1. **Efficiency:**

   - Robots operate continuously, managing inventory and preparing orders faster than human workers.

2. **Accuracy:**

   - Automated systems minimize errors in order picking and inventory management, ensuring customers receive the correct items.

3. **Scalability:**

   - Robotics systems can easily scale to handle increasing volumes of goods without significant additional labor costs.

4. **Cost Reduction:**

   - While initial investments are substantial, robots reduce long-term labor costs and increase throughput, leading to overall cost savings.

5. **Safety:**

   - Robots handle heavy lifting and repetitive tasks, reducing workplace injuries and improving worker safety.

Key Applications of Autonomous Robots in Logistics

1. **Warehouse Management:**

   o Robots navigate warehouses to retrieve items, transport goods, and manage inventory, streamlining operations.

2. **Order Picking:**

   o Autonomous robots pick items for orders with high speed and precision, improving order fulfillment rates.

3. **Automated Guided Vehicles (AGVs):**

   o AGVs transport materials across the warehouse, reducing the need for manual forklifts and enhancing workflow efficiency.

4. **Last-Mile Delivery:**

   o Robots and drones handle the final leg of delivery, bringing packages directly to customers' doorsteps efficiently and reliably.

Analogy: Think of an autonomous warehouse as a well-orchestrated symphony, where each robot plays a specific instrument, contributing to a harmonious and efficient logistics process.

Case Study: Last-Mile Delivery Solutions

Last-mile delivery—the final step in the delivery process from a distribution center to the end customer—is often the most challenging and costly part of the logistics chain. However, **Last-Mile Delivery Robots** are poised to revolutionize this segment by enhancing efficiency, reducing costs, and improving customer satisfaction.

Background

With the exponential growth of e-commerce, the demand for swift and reliable last-mile delivery has surged. Traditional delivery methods involve significant labor costs, time consumption, and susceptibility to human error or delays. Autonomous delivery robots offer a promising solution to these challenges by providing a scalable, efficient, and cost-effective means of delivering goods directly to consumers.

Implementation

1. **Design and Development:**
   - Companies like **Starship Technologies**, **Amazon Robotics**, and **Nuro** have developed compact, autonomous robots designed for sidewalk and road navigation.

2. **Navigation and Localization:**
   - Robots use a combination of GPS, LIDAR, cameras, and advanced algorithms to navigate complex urban environments, avoid obstacles, and reach delivery destinations accurately.

3. **Delivery Mechanism:**

o Equipped with secure compartments, robots safely store and transport packages, ensuring they remain intact and secure until delivered.

4. **User Interaction:**

o Customers receive notifications upon delivery, and robots can interact with users through mobile apps or interfaces to confirm identity and ensure safe delivery.

5. **Regulatory Compliance:**

o Companies work closely with local authorities to ensure robots comply with traffic laws, sidewalk regulations, and safety standards.

Outcomes

1. **Reduced Delivery Costs:**

o Autonomous robots eliminate the need for human couriers, significantly lowering labor costs associated with last-mile delivery.

2. **Increased Efficiency:**

o Robots can operate continuously, delivering packages faster and more consistently than human couriers.

3. **Enhanced Customer Satisfaction:**

- ○ Quick and reliable delivery times improve customer experiences, fostering loyalty and encouraging repeat business.

4. **Environmental Benefits:**

- ○ Electric-powered delivery robots reduce carbon emissions compared to traditional delivery vehicles, contributing to greener urban environments.

Challenges and Solutions

1. **Navigational Obstacles:**

- ○ **Challenge:** Robots must navigate complex environments with pedestrians, vehicles, and varying terrains.

- ○ **Solution:** Advanced sensor suites and AI-driven navigation algorithms enable robots to detect and avoid obstacles effectively.

2. **Weather Conditions:**

- ○ **Challenge:** Adverse weather can impair robot performance and reliability.

- ○ **Solution:** Designing weather-resistant robots with robust sealing, heating, and cooling systems ensures functionality in diverse weather conditions.

3. **Security and Theft:**

- o **Challenge:** Ensuring that packages are delivered securely without theft or tampering.

- o **Solution:** Implementing secure locking mechanisms and real-time monitoring systems enhances package security.

4. **Regulatory Hurdles:**

- o **Challenge:** Navigating varying local regulations and obtaining necessary permissions.

- o **Solution:** Collaborating with local governments and adapting robot designs to meet specific regulatory requirements facilitates smoother deployments.

Future Prospects

Last-mile delivery robots are continually evolving, with future advancements promising even greater efficiency and integration into smart city infrastructures.

1. **Enhanced Autonomy:**

- o Future robots will possess improved AI capabilities, enabling them to navigate more complex environments and handle unexpected scenarios with minimal human intervention.

2. **Integration with Smart Cities:**

- o Robots will seamlessly integrate with smart city systems, utilizing real-time traffic data, public transportation schedules, and urban infrastructure to optimize delivery routes and times.

3. **Scalability and Fleet Management:**

   o Advanced fleet management software will coordinate large numbers of delivery robots, ensuring optimal distribution and task allocation across vast geographic areas.

4. **Hybrid Delivery Models:**

   o Combining autonomous robots with traditional delivery methods can create hybrid models that maximize efficiency and coverage, addressing a wider range of delivery needs.

Conclusion of Case Study:

Last-mile delivery robots represent a significant leap forward in the logistics industry. By enhancing efficiency, reducing costs, and improving customer satisfaction, these robots are set to become a staple in modern delivery systems, shaping the future of how goods reach consumers.

Space Exploration

Robots for Extraterrestrial Missions

Imagine robots traversing the rugged terrains of Mars or exploring the icy moons of Jupiter, gathering data and performing tasks in environments too harsh for humans.

Robots for Extraterrestrial Missions are at the forefront of space exploration, enabling humanity to extend its reach beyond Earth's confines.

Importance of Robotics in Space Exploration

1. **Safety:**

   o Robots operate in environments that are hostile and unsafe for humans, protecting human lives by performing risky tasks.

2. **Extended Reach:**

   o Robots can explore distant and inaccessible regions of space, collecting valuable data and expanding our understanding of the universe.

3. **Cost Efficiency:**

   o Utilizing robots reduces the need for expensive human missions, making space exploration more sustainable and economically viable.

4. **Continuous Operation:**

   o Robots can function autonomously over extended periods, conducting experiments and gathering data without the need for constant human oversight.

Key Roles of Robots in Space Missions

1. **Surface Exploration:**

   - Robots like rovers traverse planetary surfaces, analyzing soil, rocks, and atmospheric conditions.

2. **Maintenance and Repair:**

   - Autonomous robots assist in maintaining and repairing space stations or satellites, ensuring their functionality.

3. **Sample Collection:**

   - Robots collect samples from various celestial bodies, transporting them back to designated collection points or spacecraft.

4. **Scientific Research:**

   - Robots conduct experiments in situ, providing insights into extraterrestrial environments and contributing to scientific knowledge.

Analogy: Think of extraterrestrial robots as pioneers on the frontier of space, charting unknown territories and laying the groundwork for future human exploration.

Case Study: Mars Rover Technologies

The Mars Rover missions stand as a testament to the incredible capabilities of robotic technology in space exploration. These rovers have been instrumental in advancing our understanding of the Red Planet, paving the way for future manned missions.

Background

NASA's Mars Rover program aims to explore the Martian surface, analyze its geology, search for signs of past life, and assess the planet's habitability for future human settlers. Rovers like **Sojourner**, **Spirit and Opportunity**, and **Curiosity** have each contributed uniquely to these goals.

Implementation

1. **Design and Engineering:**

   - Mars rovers are designed to withstand extreme temperatures, radiation, and rugged terrains.

   - They incorporate robust mobility systems with wheels or tracks to navigate diverse landscapes.

2. **Autonomous Navigation:**

   - Equipped with advanced sensors (LIDAR, cameras) and AI algorithms, rovers can autonomously navigate obstacles and plan paths without real-time human intervention.

3. **Scientific Instruments:**

   - Each rover carries a suite of scientific instruments, such as spectrometers, drills, and cameras, to conduct experiments and gather data.

4. **Communication Systems:**

   o Rovers communicate with Earth via orbiters, ensuring a reliable data transmission link despite the vast distances.

5. **Power Management:**

   o Solar panels or radioisotope thermoelectric generators (RTGs) provide the necessary power for rover operations.

Outcomes

1. **Geological Discoveries:**

   o Rovers have uncovered evidence of past water activity on Mars, including dried-up riverbeds and mineral deposits.

2. **Search for Life:**

   o Missions like **Opportunity** have provided crucial data suggesting that Mars once had conditions suitable for microbial life.

3. **Atmospheric Analysis:**

   o Rovers analyze the Martian atmosphere, studying its composition, weather patterns, and seasonal changes.

4. **Technology Demonstration:**

o   Each rover mission serves as a platform for testing and refining technologies for future manned missions.

Challenges and Solutions

1. **Harsh Environment:**

    o   **Challenge:** Mars' extreme temperatures and radiation levels.

    o   **Solution:** Utilize durable materials, thermal insulation, and radiation-resistant components in rover design.

2. **Communication Delays:**

    o   **Challenge:** Significant time lag between Earth and Mars complicates real-time control.

    o   **Solution:** Implement autonomous navigation and decision-making capabilities, allowing rovers to operate independently.

3. **Terrain Navigation:**

    o   **Challenge:** Navigating rocky and uneven Martian terrain.

    o   **Solution:** Advanced mobility systems with adaptive suspension and obstacle detection sensors enable effective navigation.

4. **Power Constraints:**

- ○ **Challenge:** Limited power availability due to Mars' distance from the Sun and dust accumulation on solar panels.

- ○ **Solution:** Employ RTGs for sustained power and incorporate self-cleaning mechanisms for solar panels.

Future Prospects

The success of Mars Rover missions has laid the groundwork for more ambitious projects, including:

1. **Next-Generation Rovers:**

   - ○ Future rovers will feature enhanced autonomy, greater payload capacity, and advanced scientific instruments for more comprehensive exploration.

2. **Human-Robot Collaboration:**

   - ○ Robots will assist astronauts in tasks like habitat construction, resource extraction, and scientific research, enhancing the efficiency and safety of human missions.

3. **Sample Return Missions:**

   - ○ Future rovers will collect and cache Martian samples for retrieval and analysis on Earth, providing deeper insights into the planet's history and potential for life.

4. **Interplanetary Communication:**

    o Advances in communication technologies will reduce data transmission delays, enabling more interactive and real-time control of robotic missions.

Conclusion of Case Study:

Mars Rover technologies epitomize the remarkable achievements of robotics in space exploration. These rovers not only expand our knowledge of Mars but also demonstrate the resilience and adaptability of robotic systems in the most challenging environments. As we continue to push the boundaries of exploration, the lessons learned from Mars Rovers will inform and inspire future missions, bringing us closer to unraveling the mysteries of the cosmos.

Conclusion

In this chapter, we've journeyed through the tangible impacts of autonomous robotics across various industries, from manufacturing and healthcare to logistics and space exploration. Through detailed explanations and compelling case studies, you've seen how robots are not just theoretical constructs but real-world tools transforming operations, enhancing precision, and improving lives.

Key Takeaways:

1. **Manufacturing:**

- o Robotics in manufacturing, particularly robotic arms in assembly lines, have revolutionized production efficiency, precision, and safety, setting new standards in industrial automation.

2. Healthcare:

- o Assistive robots and surgical automation are reshaping healthcare, offering enhanced patient care, improved surgical outcomes, and supporting rehabilitation efforts with unprecedented precision and adaptability.

3. Logistics:

- o Autonomous warehousing and last-mile delivery robots are streamlining supply chains, reducing costs, and meeting the high demands of modern e-commerce with efficiency and reliability.

4. Space Exploration:

- o Robots like Mars Rovers are pioneering extraterrestrial missions, expanding our understanding of other planets, and paving the way for future human exploration beyond Earth.

Next Steps:

1. Deep Dive into Specific Industries:

- o Explore more in-depth applications and emerging trends in industries like agriculture, mining, and entertainment, where robotics are making significant strides.

2. **Advanced Robotics Technologies:**

   o Investigate cutting-edge technologies such as soft robotics, bio-inspired robots, and humanoid robots, and their potential applications.

3. **Integration and Interoperability:**

   o Learn about integrating robotic systems with other technologies like IoT, AI, and big data analytics to create more intelligent and interconnected systems.

4. **Ethical and Societal Implications:**

   o Consider the ethical considerations and societal impacts of widespread robotics adoption, including job displacement, privacy concerns, and the need for regulatory frameworks.

Remember: The integration of robotics into real-world applications is an ongoing evolution. By understanding their current applications and learning from successful case studies, you're better equipped to innovate and contribute to the future of autonomous robotics.

You're now ready to harness the power of robotics to transform industries, enhance human capabilities, and explore the vast expanse of space! Embrace the challenges, stay curious, and continue building on the knowledge gained to create groundbreaking robotic solutions that shape our world.

Chapter 10: Troubleshooting and Optimization

Every robotics project, no matter how well-planned, encounters hurdles along the way. Whether you're a seasoned engineer or just starting out, understanding **Troubleshooting and Optimization** is crucial to ensure your robot operates smoothly, efficiently, and reliably. Have you ever wondered why your robot suddenly stops responding or how to make it move faster without draining its battery? This chapter demystifies common challenges in robotics projects and provides actionable strategies to overcome them. We'll delve into hardware failures, software bugs, and integration issues, explore debugging techniques tailored for ROS2 and Python, and uncover best practices for optimizing your robot's performance. Ready to transform obstacles into opportunities for improvement? Let's embark on this journey of making your robotic creations robust and high-performing!

Common Challenges in Robotics Projects

Robotics is an interdisciplinary field, combining elements of mechanical engineering, electrical engineering, and computer science. Naturally, this complexity introduces a variety of challenges that can impede progress. Understanding these common hurdles is the first step toward effectively addressing them.

1. Hardware Failures

Hardware failures are among the most common issues faced in robotics. These can range from minor glitches to complete system breakdowns.

- **Mechanical Wear and Tear:**
  - Moving parts like motors, gears, and joints are subject to wear and tear over time.
  - **Solution:** Regular maintenance and timely replacement of worn components can extend the lifespan of your robot.

- **Electrical Issues:**
  - Problems such as short circuits, power surges, or faulty wiring can disrupt the robot's functionality.
  - **Solution:** Implement robust electrical designs with proper insulation and surge protection. Use quality components to minimize failures.

- **Sensor Malfunctions:**

  - Sensors are critical for a robot's perception. Faulty sensors can lead to inaccurate data and erratic behavior.

  - **Solution:** Calibrate sensors regularly and use redundancy where possible to ensure reliability.

2. Software Bugs

Software bugs can cause unexpected behavior, crashes, or complete system failures in your robot's operations.

- **Code Errors:**

  - Syntax errors, logical flaws, or unhandled exceptions can disrupt the robot's functionality.

  - **Solution:** Adopt good coding practices, including code reviews, unit testing, and using version control systems like Git.

- **Integration Problems:**

  - Integrating various software components, libraries, and APIs can lead to compatibility issues.

  - **Solution:** Use consistent software environments and dependency management tools like Docker or virtual environments to minimize conflicts.

- **Real-Time Processing Issues:**

- o Robotics applications often require real-time data processing. Delays or lags can impact performance.

- o **Solution:** Optimize algorithms for speed and efficiency, and use real-time operating systems (RTOS) if necessary.

3. Integration Issues

Integrating hardware and software components seamlessly is a significant challenge in robotics.

- **Communication Failures:**

  - o Miscommunication between different parts of the system can lead to errors and inefficiencies.

  - o **Solution:** Implement robust communication protocols and thorough testing to ensure all components interact correctly.

- **Synchronization Problems:**

  - o Ensuring that all components operate in sync is crucial for coordinated actions.

  - o **Solution:** Use synchronization mechanisms like mutexes, semaphores, and proper timing strategies to manage concurrent operations.

- **Compatibility Concerns:**

- ○ Different components may have varying requirements and specifications, leading to compatibility issues.

- ○ **Solution:** Standardize interfaces and use middleware like ROS2 to facilitate smooth integration across diverse components.

Debugging Techniques for ROS2 and Python

When issues arise, effective debugging is essential to identify and resolve problems swiftly. ROS2 (Robot Operating System 2) paired with Python offers a powerful ecosystem for developing and debugging robotic applications.

1. Debugging in ROS2

ROS2 provides a suite of tools designed to help developers troubleshoot and optimize their robotic systems.

- **ros2 topic echo:**
  - ○ **Purpose:** Monitor messages being published on a specific topic.
  - ○ **Usage:** Helps verify if messages are being correctly sent and received.
  - ○ **Example:**

```bash
bash
```

```bash
ros2 topic echo /sensor_data
```

- **ros2 node info:**

  - ○ **Purpose:** Retrieve detailed information about a specific node.

  - ○ **Usage:** Useful for checking node status, publishers, subscribers, and parameters.

  - ○ **Example:**

- **rviz2:**

  - ○ **Purpose:** Visualization tool for ROS2, allowing real-time monitoring of sensor data, robot state, and more.

  - ○ **Usage:** Helps in diagnosing issues related to perception and navigation.

  - ○ **Example:**

```bash
bash
```

```bash
rviz2
```

- **ros2 run rqt_graph rqt_graph:**

  - ○ **Purpose:** Visualize the node and topic connections within your ROS2 system.

- o **Usage:** Identifies communication issues and ensures proper node interactions.

- o **Example:**

```bash
bash
```

```bash
ros2 run rqt_graph rqt_graph
```

2. Debugging in Python

Python is widely used in robotics for its simplicity and flexibility. Effective debugging in Python is crucial for maintaining robust code.

- **Using Debuggers:**

  - o **pdb (Python Debugger):**

    - **Purpose:** Interactive debugging tool for stepping through code, inspecting variables, and evaluating expressions.

    - **Usage:**

```python
python
```

```python
import pdb; pdb.set_trace()
```

  - o **Integrated Development Environments (IDEs):**

    - **Examples:** PyCharm, VSCode, and Eclipse with PyDev.

    - **Features:** Breakpoints, step-through execution, variable inspection, and more.

- **Logging:**

  - ○ **Purpose:** Record runtime information to diagnose issues without interrupting program flow.

  - ○ **Usage:** Utilize Python's built-in logging module to log messages at various severity levels (DEBUG, INFO, WARNING, ERROR, CRITICAL).

  - ○ **Example:**

```python
import logging

logging.basicConfig(level=logging.DEBUG)
logger = logging.getLogger(__name__)

logger.debug('This is a debug message')
logger.info('This is an info message')
```

- **Unit Testing:**

  - ○ **Purpose:** Validate individual components to ensure they work as intended.

  - ○ **Usage:** Use frameworks like unittest or pytest to write and run tests.

  - ○ **Example:**

```python
import unittest

class TestMathOperations(unittest.TestCase):
    def test_addition(self):
        self.assertEqual(1 + 1, 2)


if __name__ == '__main__':
    unittest.main()
```

Static Code Analysis:

- **Purpose:** Detect potential errors and enforce coding standards without executing the code.

- **Tools:** flake8, pylint, and mypy for type checking.

- **Usage:**

```bash
flake8 your_script.py
pylint your_script.py
mypy your_script.py
```

Tools and Best Practices

Effective troubleshooting and optimization require not just the right tools but also adherence to best practices that streamline the process and enhance productivity.

1. Essential Tools for Robotics Development

- **ROS2 Tools:**

    o **rviz2:** Visualization tool for real-time monitoring.

    o **rqt_graph:** Visualizes node and topic connections.

    o **ros2 bag:** Records and plays back ROS2 topics for testing and debugging.

- **Python Development Tools:**

    o **IDEs:** PyCharm, VSCode for enhanced coding experience.

    o **Debuggers:** pdb for interactive debugging.

    o **Testing Frameworks:** unittest, pytest for unit testing.

    o **Static Analyzers:** flake8, pylint for code quality.

- **Version Control:**

    o **Git:** Track changes, collaborate with team members, and manage code versions.

- o **Platforms:** GitHub, GitLab, Bitbucket for repository hosting.

- **Simulation Environments:**

  - o **Gazebo:** Simulates complex robotic environments for testing.

  - o **Webots:** Another powerful simulator for robotics research and development.

2. Best Practices for Effective Troubleshooting

- **Systematic Approach:**

  - o Break down the problem into smaller, manageable components.

  - o Test each component individually to isolate the issue.

- **Documentation:**

  - o Maintain detailed documentation of your system architecture, configurations, and changes.

  - o Document encountered issues and their solutions for future reference.

- **Regular Testing:**

  - o Implement continuous integration and continuous deployment (CI/CD) pipelines to automate testing.

- Perform regular unit tests and integration tests to catch issues early.

- **Collaboration and Communication:**

  - Use collaborative tools like Slack, Microsoft Teams, or Trello to communicate with team members.

  - Share findings and solutions to foster a collaborative troubleshooting environment.

- **Version Control Discipline:**

  - Commit changes frequently with clear, descriptive messages.

  - Use branching strategies (e.g., Gitflow) to manage different development stages.

Optimizing Performance

Optimization ensures that your robot operates at peak performance, balancing speed, efficiency, and resource utilization. Let's explore strategies to enhance your robot's efficiency and responsiveness, along with effective resource management techniques.

1. Enhancing Efficiency and Responsiveness

- **Algorithm Optimization:**

  - **Profiling Code:**

- Identify performance bottlenecks using profiling tools like cProfile or line_profiler.

- **Example:**

```python
import cProfile

def compute():
    # Intensive computation
    pass

cProfile.run('compute()')
```

- **Algorithm Selection:**

  - Choose the most efficient algorithms suited to your task. For instance, use A^* for pathfinding instead of Dijkstra's if heuristics can be applied.

- **Code Optimization:**

  - Refactor code to eliminate redundancies, use vectorized operations with NumPy, and leverage efficient data structures.

- **Parallel Processing:**

  - **Multithreading and Multiprocessing:**

- Utilize Python's threading and multiprocessing modules to perform concurrent tasks.

- **Example:**

```python

import multiprocessing

def task():
    # Perform a CPU-bound task
    pass

if __name__ == '__main__':
    processes = []
    for _ in range(4):
        p = multiprocessing.Process(target=task)
        p.start()
        processes.append(p)
```

for p in processes:
```python
        p.join()
```

- **Asynchronous Programming:**

- Use asyncio for I/O-bound tasks to improve responsiveness without blocking.

- **Example:**

```python
```

```
import asyncio

async def fetch_data():
    # Simulate I/O-bound task
    await asyncio.sleep(1)
    return "Data"

async def main():
    result = await fetch_data()
    print(result)

asyncio.run(main())
```

- **Hardware Acceleration:**

  o **GPUs and TPUs:**

    - Offload intensive computations to GPUs or TPUs using libraries like TensorFlow or PyTorch for tasks like image processing or neural network inference.

  o **FPGA Integration:**

    - Use Field-Programmable Gate Arrays (FPGAs) for custom, high-speed processing tasks.

2. Resource Management Strategies

Efficient resource management ensures that your robot makes the best use of its limited resources, such as CPU, memory, and power.

- **Memory Management:**
  - ○ **Avoid Memory Leaks:**
    - ▪ Ensure that objects are properly deleted and resources are released when no longer needed.
  - ○ **Use Efficient Data Structures:**
    - ▪ Choose data structures that minimize memory usage, such as using generators instead of lists for large datasets.
  - ○ **Example:**

python

```python
def data_generator():
    for i in range(1000000):
        yield i

for data in data_generator():
    process(data)
```

- **Power Optimization:**
  - ○ **Energy-Efficient Components:**

- Select hardware components that consume less power without compromising performance.

  o **Dynamic Power Management:**

    - Implement strategies to scale CPU frequency or deactivate unused components to save power.

  o **Sleep Modes:**

    - Utilize sleep modes when the robot is idle to conserve energy.

- **CPU and GPU Utilization:**

  o **Load Balancing:**

    - Distribute computational tasks evenly across available CPU cores or GPU units to prevent overloading any single resource.

  o **Task Scheduling:**

    - Prioritize critical tasks and schedule less urgent ones during periods of low activity.

- **Real-Time Resource Allocation:**

  o **Monitoring Tools:**

    - Use tools like htop, nvidia-smi, or ROS2's built-in monitoring tools to track resource usage in real-time.

- o **Dynamic Adjustment:**
  - Adjust resource allocation based on current load and performance requirements.

Hands-On Project: Optimizing Your Robot's Performance

Optimization is an ongoing process that involves continuously assessing and improving your robot's performance. In this hands-on project, you'll apply the strategies discussed to identify and eliminate bottlenecks, ensuring your robot operates efficiently and responsively.

Step 1: Setting Up Your Environment

Before diving into optimization, ensure your development environment is properly set up.

1. **Ensure ROS2 is Installed and Configured:**
   - o Follow the official ROS2 installation guide to set up ROS2 on your system.
2. **Set Up a Python Virtual Environment:**
   - o **Action:**

bash

```
python3 -m venv robot_env
```

```
source robot_env/bin/activate
pip install -r requirements.txt  # Install
necessary packages
```

3. **Install Necessary Tools:**

        ○ **Action:**

```bash
pip install numpy pandas tensorflow pytest flake8
sudo apt install python3-pip ros-humble-rqt-graph
ros-humble-ros2bag
```

Step 2: Profiling Your Robot's Code

Identifying where your robot is spending the most time is crucial for effective optimization.

1. **Use cProfile to Profile Your Python Code:**

        ○ **Action:**

```python
import cProfile

def robot_main():
    # Your robot's main loop
    pass

if __name__ == '__main__':
    cProfile.run('robot_main()')
```

2. **Analyze the Profiling Results:**

  o Look for functions with the highest cumulative time.

  o Identify inefficient loops, unnecessary computations, or blocking operations.

Step 3: Monitoring System Resources

Understanding how your robot utilizes system resources helps in managing them effectively.

1. **Monitor CPU and Memory Usage with htop:**

  o **Action:**

```bash
```

```bash
htop
```

2. **Check GPU Utilization with nvidia-smi (if applicable):**

  o **Action:**

```bash
```

```bash
nvidia-smi
```

3. **Use ROS2 Tools to Monitor Topics and Nodes:**

  o **Action:**

```bash
```

```
ros2 run rqt_graph rqt_graph
ros2 topic hz /sensor_data
```

Step 4: Implementing Code Optimizations

With bottlenecks identified, proceed to optimize your code.

1. **Refactor Inefficient Code:**

   o   Replace nested loops with vectorized operations.

   o   Example:

```python
import numpy as np

# Inefficient loop
data = [i for i in range(1000000)]
result = []
for i in data:
    result.append(i * 2)

# Optimized with NumPy
data_np = np.array(data)
result_np = data_np * 2
```

2. **Implement Parallel Processing:**

   o   **Action:**

```python
import multiprocessing
```

```python
def process_sensor_data(data):
    # Intensive processing
    return [d * 2 for d in data]


if __name__ == '__main__':
    data = list(range(1000000))
    chunks = [data[x:x+100000] for x in range(0,
len(data), 100000)]
    with multiprocessing.Pool() as pool:
        results = pool.map(process_sensor_data,
chunks)
    data_processed = [item for sublist in results
for item in sublist]
```

3. Leverage GPU Acceleration for Deep Learning Tasks:

   ○ **Action:**

```python
python


import tensorflow as tf


with tf.device('/GPU:0'):
    model = tf.keras.models.Sequential([
        tf.keras.layers.Dense(128,
activation='relu'),
        tf.keras.layers.Dense(10,
activation='softmax')
    ])
```

```
model.compile(optimizer='adam',

loss='categorical_crossentropy',
              metrics=['accuracy'])
# Train the model on GPU
model.fit(x_train, y_train, epochs=10)
```

Step 5: Optimizing ROS2 Nodes

Ensure that your ROS2 nodes are running efficiently to minimize communication delays and resource usage.

1. **Reduce Topic Publishing Rates for Non-Critical Data:**

   o **Action:**

```python
self.create_timer(0.5, self.publish_sensor_data)
# Reduce from 1 Hz to 2 Hz
```

2. **Merge Multiple Nodes into a Single Node:**

   o **Action:**

      - Combine related functionalities to reduce inter-node communication overhead.

      - Example: Combine sensor data processing and control commands into one node.

3. **Optimize Message Handling:**

   o Use lightweight message types and compress data where possible.

○ **Action:**

```python
from std_msgs.msg import String
import zlib


class OptimizedPublisher(Node):
    def __init__(self):
        super().__init__('optimized_publisher')
        self.publisher = self.create_publisher(String, 'compressed_data', 10)
        self.timer = self.create_timer(1.0, self.publish_data)

    def publish_data(self):
        data = b'This is some data to compress'
        compressed = zlib.compress(data)
        msg = String()
        msg.data = compressed.decode('latin1')  # Encoding binary data as string
        self.publisher.publish(msg)
```

Step 6: Testing and Validation

After implementing optimizations, validate that performance improvements are realized without introducing new issues.

1. **Run Profiling Again:**

- o **Action:**

```python
python
```

```python
cProfile.run('robot_main()')
```

2. **Monitor Resource Usage:**

- o **Action:**

```bash
bash
```

```bash
htop
nvidia-smi
```

3. **Perform Functional Testing:**

   - o Ensure that all robot functionalities operate correctly and efficiently.

   - o Use ROS2's ros2 topic echo and rviz2 to verify data flows.

4. **Gather Feedback:**

   - o Collect performance metrics and user feedback to assess the effectiveness of optimizations.

Summary

In Chapter 10, "Troubleshooting and Optimization," we explored the common challenges encountered in robotics projects, including hardware failures, software bugs, and integration issues. By understanding these obstacles, you can better prepare to address them effectively. We delved into debugging techniques tailored for ROS2 and Python, leveraging tools like cProfile, rviz2, and Python's logging module to identify and resolve issues efficiently.

The chapter also covered essential tools and best practices for maintaining robust robotic systems, emphasizing the importance of systematic approaches, regular testing, and effective documentation. Moving into optimization, we discussed strategies to enhance your robot's efficiency and responsiveness, such as algorithm optimization, parallel processing, and hardware acceleration. Additionally, we highlighted resource management techniques to ensure your robot makes the most of its CPU, memory, and power resources.

Through a comprehensive hands-on project, you applied these optimization strategies to identify performance bottlenecks in your robot's system and implement targeted solutions. This practical application not only reinforced the concepts discussed but also provided you with the confidence to tackle real-world performance issues in your own projects.

Key Takeaways:

1. **Common Challenges:**

   - Hardware failures, software bugs, and integration issues are prevalent in robotics projects.

   - Proactive maintenance and robust design can mitigate many hardware-related problems.

2. **Debugging Techniques:**

- o Utilize ROS2's suite of tools for monitoring and visualization.

- o Employ Python's debugging tools, such as pdb and logging, to troubleshoot software issues effectively.

3. **Tools and Best Practices:**

- o Adopt a systematic approach to troubleshooting, incorporating regular testing and thorough documentation.

- o Leverage collaborative tools and version control systems to streamline development and troubleshooting processes.

4. **Optimizing Performance:**

- o Profile your code to identify inefficiencies and optimize algorithms for better performance.

- o Implement parallel processing and hardware acceleration to handle intensive tasks more efficiently.

5. **Resource Management:**

- o Efficiently manage CPU, memory, and power resources to ensure your robot operates smoothly.

- Use monitoring tools to track resource usage and adjust allocations dynamically.

6. **Hands-On Project:**

- Identifying and addressing performance bottlenecks through profiling and targeted optimizations can significantly enhance your robot's efficiency and responsiveness.

By mastering troubleshooting and optimization, you equip yourself with the skills to create more reliable, efficient, and high-performing robotic systems. These capabilities are essential for advancing your robotics projects and overcoming the inevitable challenges that arise during development and deployment.

Chapter 11: Future Trends in Autonomous Robotics

Welcome to **Future Trends in Autonomous Robotics**, where we peer into the horizon to explore the cutting-edge advancements set to redefine the landscape of robotics. Have you ever wondered what the next generation of robots will look like or how emerging technologies will shape their capabilities? From leaps in artificial intelligence to groundbreaking sensor innovations and the evolution of ROS2, the future of autonomous robotics is both exciting and transformative. This chapter delves into these emerging technologies, examines the future trajectory of ROS2, and provides strategies to prepare for the ever-evolving robotic ecosystem. Ready to envision the robots of tomorrow? Let's embark on this forward-looking journey!

Emerging Technologies

Autonomous robotics is a rapidly advancing field, continuously fueled by breakthroughs in various technological domains. Staying abreast of these emerging technologies is crucial for developers, engineers, and enthusiasts aiming to harness the full potential of robotics.

Advances in AI and Machine Learning

Artificial Intelligence (AI) and Machine Learning (ML) are the lifeblood of modern autonomous robotics, enabling robots to perceive, learn, and make decisions with increasing sophistication.

Key Developments:

1. **Deep Learning Enhancements:**

   - **Description:** Deep learning models, particularly Convolutional Neural Networks (CNNs) and Recurrent Neural Networks (RNNs), have become more efficient and accurate.

   - **Impact:** Improved object recognition, scene understanding, and predictive analytics empower robots to navigate and interact with their environments more effectively.

2. **Reinforcement Learning:**

   - **Description:** Robots learn optimal behaviors through trial and error by receiving feedback from their actions.

   - **Impact:** Enables autonomous decision-making in complex and dynamic environments, enhancing adaptability and performance.

3. **Transfer Learning:**

- o **Description:** Models trained on one task are adapted to perform related tasks with minimal additional training.

- o **Impact:** Reduces the time and data required to train robots for new tasks, accelerating deployment and versatility.

4. **Natural Language Processing (NLP):**

   - o **Description:** Advances in NLP allow robots to understand and generate human language more accurately.

   - o **Impact:** Facilitates more intuitive human-robot interactions, enabling robots to comprehend instructions, answer questions, and engage in meaningful dialogues.

Innovations in Sensor Technology

Sensors are the eyes and ears of robots, enabling them to perceive and interact with their surroundings. Innovations in sensor technology are pivotal for enhancing robotic capabilities.

Key Innovations:

1. **LiDAR (Light Detection and Ranging):**

   - o **Description:** Uses laser pulses to create detailed 3D maps of environments.

- o **Impact:** Enhances navigation and obstacle avoidance, especially in autonomous vehicles and drones.

2. **Advanced Cameras and Vision Systems:**

   - o **Description:** High-resolution cameras combined with depth sensors and thermal imaging.

   - o **Impact:** Improves object detection, recognition, and situational awareness, enabling robots to perform complex tasks like surveillance and inspection.

3. **Tactile Sensors:**

   - o **Description:** Provide robots with a sense of touch, detecting pressure, texture, and temperature.

   - o **Impact:** Enables delicate manipulation tasks, such as handling fragile objects or performing precise assembly.

4. **Multi-Sensor Fusion:**

   - o **Description:** Integrates data from multiple sensors to create a comprehensive understanding of the environment.

   - o **Impact:** Enhances accuracy and reliability in perception, decision-making, and autonomous navigation.

The Future of ROS2

ROS2 (Robot Operating System 2) is the backbone of many robotic systems, providing a flexible framework for building complex applications. The future of ROS2 is poised for significant enhancements, driven by community contributions and technological advancements.

Upcoming Features and Enhancements:

1. **Real-Time Capabilities:**

   - **Description:** Enhancing ROS2's ability to handle real-time processing.

   - **Impact:** Enables time-critical applications, such as autonomous driving and real-time data analysis.

2. **Improved Security:**

   - **Description:** Incorporating robust security measures to protect against cyber threats.

   - **Impact:** Ensures safe and secure operation of robots in sensitive and critical environments.

3. **Enhanced Middleware Support:**

   - **Description:** Expanding support for various middleware solutions to improve communication efficiency.

   - **Impact:** Facilitates better interoperability and performance across different robotic platforms.

4. **Advanced Simulation Tools:**

   o **Description:** Integrating more sophisticated simulation environments within ROS2.

   o **Impact:** Provides developers with more accurate and realistic testing scenarios, reducing development time and costs.

5. **AI and ML Integration:**

   o **Description:** Seamlessly integrating AI and ML libraries and frameworks.

   o **Impact:** Simplifies the deployment of intelligent behaviors and learning capabilities in robots.

Community and Ecosystem Growth

The ROS2 community is a vibrant and collaborative ecosystem that plays a crucial role in its evolution.

Key Aspects:

1. **Open-Source Contributions:**

   o **Description:** Encouraging developers worldwide to contribute code, documentation, and tools.

   o **Impact:** Accelerates the development of new features and improvements, fostering innovation.

2. **Educational Initiatives:**

- ○ **Description:** Expanding ROS2 education through tutorials, workshops, and online courses.

- ○ **Impact:** Increases accessibility and skill development, empowering more individuals to engage in robotics development.

3. **Industry Partnerships:**

- ○ **Description:** Collaborating with industry leaders to integrate ROS2 into commercial products and services.

- ○ **Impact:** Enhances ROS2's applicability and drives its adoption in various sectors.

4. **Tooling and Libraries:**

- ○ **Description:** Developing and maintaining a rich set of tools and libraries to support diverse robotic applications.

- ○ **Impact:** Simplifies the development process and expands the range of possible applications.

Preparing for the Future

As the field of autonomous robotics continues to evolve, staying prepared for upcoming technological changes is essential. This section outlines strategies to ensure you remain at the forefront of robotics advancements.

Continuous Learning and Skill Development

The rapid pace of technological change necessitates a commitment to continuous learning. Here's how to stay updated and enhance your skill set:

Step-by-Step Approach:

1. **Enroll in Online Courses and Certifications:**

    o **Action:** Platforms like Coursera, edX, and Udacity offer specialized courses in AI, ML, ROS2, and robotics.

    o **Benefit:** Provides structured learning paths and up-to-date content from industry experts.

2. **Participate in Workshops and Webinars:**

    o **Action:** Attend events hosted by robotics organizations, universities, and tech companies.

    o **Benefit:** Gain hands-on experience and insights from leading practitioners.

3. **Engage with the Community:**

    o **Action:** Join forums, discussion groups, and social media communities focused on robotics and ROS2.

    o **Benefit:** Exchange knowledge, seek advice, and stay informed about the latest trends and challenges.

4. **Read Research Papers and Industry Publications:**

- ○ **Action:** Follow journals like IEEE Robotics and Automation Letters and platforms like arXiv.

- ○ **Benefit:** Stay abreast of cutting-edge research and emerging technologies.

5. **Build Personal Projects:**

- ○ **Action:** Apply

your learning by developing your own robotics projects or contributing to open-source projects.

- • **Benefit:** Reinforces theoretical knowledge through practical application and builds a portfolio to showcase your skills.

Adapting to Technological Changes

Embracing change is fundamental to thriving in the dynamic field of robotics. Here's how to effectively adapt:

Step-by-Step Approach:

1. **Stay Agile in Learning:**

- ○ **Action:** Be open to learning new programming languages, frameworks, and tools as they emerge.

- ○ **Benefit:** Ensures you remain versatile and capable of handling diverse projects.

2. **Foster a Growth Mindset:**

- o **Action:** View challenges and setbacks as opportunities for growth rather than obstacles.

- o **Benefit:** Enhances resilience and drives continuous improvement.

3. **Implement Feedback Loops:**

- o **Action:** Regularly seek feedback from peers, mentors, and users to identify areas for improvement.

- o **Benefit:** Facilitates iterative development and ensures your projects meet real-world needs.

4. **Leverage Modular and Scalable Designs:**

- o **Action:** Design your robotic systems with modularity and scalability in mind, allowing for easy upgrades and expansions.

- o **Benefit:** Simplifies the integration of new technologies and features without overhauling existing systems.

5. **Embrace Interdisciplinary Collaboration:**

- o **Action:** Collaborate with professionals from different fields, such as AI, mechanical engineering, and data science.

- o **Benefit:** Promotes innovative solutions and comprehensive problem-solving.

Future Trends in Autonomous Robotics

The landscape of autonomous robotics is set to undergo significant transformations driven by advancements in technology and evolving societal needs. Let's explore the key trends that will shape the future of this field.

1. Human-Robot Collaboration

Description:

The integration of robots into human-centric environments is enhancing collaboration between humans and machines. This trend focuses on creating robots that can work alongside humans safely and efficiently, complementing human skills and enhancing productivity.

Key Developments:

1. **Cobots (Collaborative Robots):**

   - **Description:** Designed to work directly with humans without the need for safety cages.

   - **Impact:** Increase flexibility in manufacturing and service industries, allowing humans and robots to perform tasks together seamlessly.

2. **Enhanced Interaction Interfaces:**

   - **Description:** Development of intuitive interfaces such as gesture recognition, voice commands, and augmented reality (AR) overlays.

- ○ **Impact:** Facilitates more natural and effective communication between humans and robots, improving task coordination.

3. **Adaptive Learning:**

- ○ **Description:** Robots equipped with adaptive learning capabilities to understand and predict human behavior.

- ○ **Impact:** Enables robots to anticipate needs and adjust their actions accordingly, enhancing efficiency and user satisfaction.

2. Autonomous Vehicles and Drones

Description:

Autonomous vehicles (AVs) and drones are revolutionizing transportation and logistics, offering unprecedented levels of efficiency, safety, and convenience. These technologies are becoming integral to various sectors, including delivery services, agriculture, and emergency response.

Key Developments:

1. **Self-Driving Cars:**

- ○ **Description:** Vehicles capable of navigating and driving without human intervention.

- ○ **Impact:** Potential to reduce traffic accidents, lower transportation costs, and provide mobility solutions for those unable to drive.

2. **Delivery Drones:**

   ○ **Description:** Unmanned aerial vehicles designed for the delivery of goods.

   ○ **Impact:** Accelerates delivery times, reduces human labor costs, and expands delivery reach to remote or hard-to-access areas.

3. **Agricultural Drones:**

   ○ **Description:** Drones used for monitoring crops, spraying pesticides, and collecting agricultural data.

   ○ **Impact:** Enhances precision farming, increases crop yields, and minimizes resource usage.

4. **Autonomous Public Transport:**

   ○ **Description:** Buses and shuttles operating without drivers.

   ○ **Impact:** Improves public transportation efficiency, reduces operational costs, and increases accessibility in urban and rural areas.

3. Soft Robotics

Description:

Soft robotics involves creating robots with flexible, compliant materials that mimic the adaptability and dexterity of living organisms. This trend is expanding the range of tasks robots can perform, particularly in delicate and intricate operations.

Key Developments:

1. **Flexible Actuators:**

    o **Description:** Actuators made from soft materials that can bend, stretch, and twist.

    o **Impact:** Enables robots to navigate complex environments and manipulate objects with varying shapes and textures.

2. **Bio-Inspired Designs:**

    o **Description:** Robots designed to emulate biological organisms, such as octopuses or insects.

    o **Impact:** Enhances maneuverability, adaptability, and efficiency in tasks requiring intricate movements.

3. **Soft Sensors:**

    o **Description:** Sensors integrated into soft materials to provide tactile feedback and environmental sensing.

    o **Impact:** Improves the robot's ability to interact safely and effectively with humans and delicate objects.

4. **Wearable Robotics:**

- ○ **Description:** Soft robotic exoskeletons and wearable devices designed to augment human capabilities.

- ○ **Impact:** Assists individuals with mobility impairments, enhances human strength and endurance, and provides support in physically demanding tasks.

4. Swarm Robotics

Description:

Swarm robotics is inspired by the collective behavior of social insects like ants and bees, where large numbers of simple robots work together to perform complex tasks. This trend focuses on creating scalable, resilient, and efficient robotic systems through decentralized control and collaboration.

Key Developments:

1. **Decentralized Control Algorithms:**

   - ○ **Description:** Algorithms that enable robots to make decisions based on local information and interactions.

   - ○ **Impact:** Enhances scalability and resilience, allowing swarms to adapt to changing environments without centralized oversight.

2. **Collaborative Task Allocation:**

o **Description:** Systems where robots autonomously assign tasks among themselves based on individual capabilities and current workload.

o **Impact:** Increases efficiency and flexibility, enabling swarms to tackle a wide range of tasks seamlessly.

3. **Communication Protocols:**

o **Description:** Robust communication methods that allow robots to share information and coordinate actions effectively.

o **Impact:** Ensures reliable collaboration and information sharing, critical for the success of swarm operations.

4. **Applications in Search and Rescue:**

o **Description:** Deploying robot swarms to locate and assist victims in disaster-stricken areas.

o **Impact:** Enhances search coverage, speed, and accuracy, improving rescue mission outcomes.

5. Edge Computing in Robotics

Description:

Edge computing involves processing data closer to the source, reducing latency and bandwidth usage compared to centralized cloud computing. This trend is crucial for real-time robotic applications that require immediate data processing and decision-making.

Key Developments:

1. **On-Device AI:**

    o **Description:** Integrating AI capabilities directly into robotic hardware.

    o **Impact:** Enables faster data processing and decision-making, essential for autonomous navigation and real-time interactions.

2. **Low-Power Computing Solutions:**

    o **Description:** Developing energy-efficient processors and hardware accelerators for edge devices.

    o **Impact:** Extends the operational time of robots, particularly in mobile and remote applications where power resources are limited.

3. **Distributed Processing Architectures:**

    o **Description:** Creating architectures where multiple edge devices collaborate to process data.

    o **Impact:** Enhances computational power and reliability, allowing robots to handle more complex tasks without relying on centralized servers.

4. **Real-Time Data Analytics:**

  - ○ **Description:** Implementing systems that analyze data instantly as it is collected.

  - ○ **Impact:** Improves the robot's ability to respond to dynamic environments and make informed decisions on the fly.

Summary

In Chapter 11, "Future Trends in Autonomous Robotics," we explored the cutting-edge advancements set to redefine the landscape of robotics. The chapter began by delving into **Emerging Technologies**, highlighting significant developments in Artificial Intelligence (AI) and Machine Learning (ML), which are enhancing robotic intelligence and decision-making capabilities. We examined innovations in sensor technology, such as advanced LiDAR systems and tactile sensors, which are improving robot perception and interaction with their environments. The evolution of **ROS2 (Robot Operating System 2)** was discussed, emphasizing upcoming features like real-time capabilities, improved security, enhanced middleware support, and the integration of AI and ML libraries, driven by a growing community and ecosystem.

The chapter also focused on key **Future Trends** shaping autonomous robotics. **Human-Robot Collaboration** is becoming more seamless with the development of cobots and enhanced interaction interfaces, allowing robots to work alongside humans safely and efficiently. **Autonomous Vehicles and Drones** are revolutionizing transportation and logistics, offering efficiency and safety improvements in sectors like delivery services and agriculture. **Soft Robotics** is expanding the range of tasks robots can perform through flexible and compliant designs, enabling delicate and complex manipulation. **Swarm Robotics** leverages decentralized control and collaboration, enabling scalable and resilient robotic systems for tasks like search and rescue. **Edge Computing** is enhancing real-time processing and decision-making, ensuring robots operate efficiently without excessive reliance on centralized systems.

Finally, the chapter provided strategies for **Preparing for the Future**, emphasizing the importance of continuous learning and skill development to stay abreast of technological advancements. It highlighted the need to adapt to technological changes through a growth mindset, feedback loops, and interdisciplinary collaboration, ensuring readiness to navigate and contribute to the evolving robotics landscape.

Through this comprehensive exploration of future trends, Chapter 11 underscored the profound and multifaceted contributions of emerging technologies to autonomous robotics, demonstrating their critical role in shaping the future of robotics across various sectors. This forward-looking perspective not only provided a deeper understanding of what lies ahead but also inspired readers to engage with and contribute to the ongoing evolution of autonomous robotics.